Navigating Big Data Analytics

Strategies for the Quality Systems Analyst

William D. Mawby

Quality Press
Milwaukee, Wisconsin

Published by ASQ Quality Press, Milwaukee, WI

© 2021 by William D. Mawby

Publisher's Cataloging-in-Publication data

Names: Mawby, William D., 1952-, author.
Title: Navigating big data analytics : strategies for the quality systems analyst / by Dr. William D. Mawby.
Description: Includes bibliographical resources. | Milwaukee, WI: Quality Press, 2021.
Identifiers: LCCN: 2021939486 | ISBN: 978-1-951058-15-9 (paperback) | 978-1-951058-16-6 (epub) | 978-1-951058-17-3 (pdf)
Subjects: LCSH Big data. | Data mining. | Quality control. | Statistics—Evaluation. | Statistics—Methodology. | BISAC COMPUTERS / Data Science / Data Analytics
Classification: LCC QA276 .M39 2021 | DDC 519.5—dc23

ASQ advances individual, organizational, and community excellence worldwide through learning, quality improvement, and knowledge exchange.

Attention bookstores, wholesalers, schools, and corporations: Quality Press books are available at quantity discounts with bulk purchases for business, trade, or educational uses. For information, please contact Quality Press at 800-248-1946 or books@asq.org.

To place orders or browse the selection of Quality Press titles, visit our website at: http://www.asq.org/quality-press

Printed in the United States of America.

25 24 23 22 21 SWY 5 4 3 2 1

Quality Press
600 N. Plankinton Ave.
Milwaukee, WI 53203-2914
Email: books@asq.org

ASQ Excellence Through Quality™

Table of Contents

Figures and Tables

Introduction

The message people are hearing today is that all data are good and the more we have of this magic stuff, the better our analyses will be. Indeed, if we follow this chain of reasoning to its logical end, then having enormously large data sets must be the answer to all our problems. At least that's what we hear from the promoters of big data analytics. The message seems to have achieved a strong level of market penetration judging by frenzied activity in the arena.[1] Who can blame the customer for accepting these claims at face value, since they seem to offer an ideal situation for companies? Who would not like to be able to glean useful information simply by looking at large data sets in clever ways? The fact that the collection of data is becoming easier and cheaper every day would seem to make this "clever" approach a no-brainer. But there might be reason to apply some judicious caution before accepting this information as truth. In this book, we will take a closer look at some of the promises of big data and how some common characteristics of the data themselves can pose challenges for an easy approach.

1

An Introduction to Big Data Analytics

Big data analytics is defined as the use of algorithms on large data sets to drive decisions that are of value to a company or organization.[2] Often the power of a big data analytics approach is emphasized by describing it as having three "V" words: *volume, velocity,* and *variety.*

- *Volume* refers to the sheer number of data points that are captured and stored. The size of the data sets that are collected can run into terabytes of information—or even larger in some cases.

- *Velocity* implies that the data are collected more frequently than they have been in the past.

- *Variety* implies that more kinds of data can be collected and used, including textual and graphical information.

We only need to look at videos that are uploaded to social media to understand the allure of using non-numeric data. The potential of using this kind of data has a rich appeal. Once these vast repositories of data are built, then the promise is that we can mine them, automatically, to detect patterns that can drive decisions to lend value to a company's activities. The applications of big data analytics run the gamut from customer management through product development through supply chain management.

Consider, for example, the kinds of applications to which big data approaches can be applied to advantage.[3]

- The Bank of England is reported to have instituted a big data approach toward the integration of various macroeconomics and microeconomics data sets to which it has access.

- General Electric has invested a lot of effort into creating systems that are efficient at analyzing sensory data so they can integrate production control.

- Xiaomi, a Chinese telephone company, has reportedly used big data to determine the right marketing strategies for its business.

Indeed, organizations that have access to substantial data are trying, in some fashion, to leverage this information to their advantage through big data approaches.

It is also possible to gain an understanding of the scope and size of these big data and data sets by looking at some examples online. Readers can access some typical public data sets that have proved to be useful in this arena.[4] Of course, most business data sets are proprietary and confidential and only accessible to those who are employed by the same companies. In this book, we will depend primarily on artificially constructed data sets in order to focus on the essentials of the problem with big data analytics to prevent us from becoming mired in the details that might be associated with other applications.

For example, the Modified National Institute of Standards and Technology (MNIST) database contains more than 60,000 examples of handwritten digits that can be used in an analysis. Internet Movie Database (IMDb) reviews can provide around 50,000 text-based movie reviews. These examples clearly show how the variety and volume of these different big data sets can be dramatic. The same features that provide big data analysis with some of its most unique applications can also make it impossible to show all the issues that are involved with such efforts.

Many purveyors of big data analysis go even further in their claims by arguing that traditional statistical analyses are likely to be inadequate when applied to very large data sets. They argue that those inadequacies necessitate the development of new data analysis approaches.[5] Most of these new analytic approaches are computationally intensive and extremely flexible in the ways you can use them to interrogate the data. The application of these new methodologies to uniquely large data sets often is accomplished through the activities of a data scientist whose skill set seems to be a combination of statistics and computer science. Job growth in the area of data science has increased in the last few decades, becoming one of the most highly sought-after positions. All this evidence seems to support the conclusion that big data is becoming essential to the operations of any modern company. It is easy to believe that solutions will appear, as if by magic, once the genie of big data is unleashed.

Deep Learning

At the leading edge of this push to leverage big data is the development of the new field of deep learning.[6] Deep learning is a direct attempt to replace human cognition with a computer[7] that usually relies on using a multilayered neural network to mimic the human brain's complex structure of synaptic connections. Although deep learning seems to be making some progress, it is nowhere near its ultimate objective to achieve strong artificial intelligence that will replace humans. The dream of artificial intelligence seems to be a world in which the human analytics practitioners have nothing to do but slowly sip their lattes while the algorithm solves all of their problems.

This book aims to address the legitimacy of the claim that big data supporters make: large data sets will be sufficient to accomplish a company's objectives. We will take a deep dive into the issues that are involved with these approaches and attempt to delineate some apparent boundaries of the big data approach. By providing detailed examples of challenges that can occur commonly in real applications of data analysis, we will belie the conclusion that simply having large data sets will ever be sufficient to replace the human analyst.

When to Use This Technology

Interest in big data has certainly not gone unnoticed by the analysts who are employed in business and industry for the twin purposes of quality and productivity. There is little doubt that most companies are trying hard to find ways to milk this promising new source of information. Anything that can be used to help in solving process problems and improving performance is always of vital interest to these sorts of professionals. Many times, however, it is not clear how to use these new techniques to gain the most value. While not an idle concern, since the speed of modern industry continues to challenge most departments, it is no wonder that many quality practitioners are tempted to think big data analysis is the answer to their prayers. It seems too good to be true that you could get so much out of so little effort. But is this a justified belief? Perhaps things are being over-marketed to some extent, and the best course is to practice caution in adopting these new approaches.

It should be made clear from the outset that this book is not trying to dispute that the use of digital computers has transformed our world in all sorts of ways. This assertion is supported by the many valuable computer algorithms that are being employed today for the purposes of selling tickets, managing sports teams, helping people find the perfect mate, and many other activities. Except for the occasional Luddite who feels that the world is spinning out of control, most people would agree that computerization makes things better. It would be the rare analytics practitioner who would be willingly to give up his or her computer. Most people are after the newest and fastest computer available, but does this practical advantage also provide evidence that is strong enough to lend credence to the extravagant claims of big data? Or could there be some instances or situations in which the naïve big data approach would not only fail to replace the human expert driven analysis, but actually could lead to subpar performance? This is an important and timely question for practitioners as they seek to forge a pathway into the future. Making the wrong decision can affect a person's analytic potential for a long time. Quality experts want to get ahead, not fall behind, in their never-ending quest for continuous improvement. The task we have in this text is to demonstrate that it is, indeed, the case that something more than just data must be used to get satisfactory results in many instances.

We are also not trying to argue that more and better data cannot be useful. Collecting more data and using them in a more automated fashion are lynchpins in the new Industry 4.0 and Quality 4.0 initiatives promoted by the American Society for Quality (ASQ) and others.[8] There is a clear benefit to be gained if we can collect pertinent data, collate them, and use them well without using up too many valuable resources. This book verifies the potential value of this approach, and, in addition, shows that understanding these data sources can be critical to obtaining their full value for the quality practitioner. Just as we need to perform due diligence while assessing and maintaining the quality of the data that are used for analysis, we also need to understand the more intimate features of the data that are caused by the details of collection and manipulation. There are many challenges that can arise when data sets become larger that must be countered to make real progress. It is the objective of this book to warn quality managers and practitioners against the naïve view that more data, by themselves, are sufficient for success. It should probably come as no surprise to veterans in this field that it is critical for human expertise to be integrated into the analysis process to be successful, even in the largest big data endeavors.

Defining the Problem

The fundamental question is whether big data, by itself, can lead to analyses that are equal, or even superior, to those made by a human analyst. Humans were able to solve complicated problems long before computers existed, so computers are not absolutely essential to problem-solving. As one example, the invention of the general-purpose digital computer itself did not require the assistance of computers. On the other hand, computers can speed up the analysis process. Even common household budgeting tasks would take orders of magnitude more time if they were done without the aid of computers. One could certainly argue that some tasks, simply because of their complexity, would not even be attempted if computers were not available to assist humans. However, it is not the practical advantages of computers that are of interest here, but rather the issue of whether big data is intrinsically equivalent to good human-based analysis. There could be some kind of technical threshold that, once passed, will enable big data alone to match the best efforts of human analysis.[9]

If and when the computer is able to produce results that equal those coming from human minds, we can also examine the interesting question of whether computers can go even further to outstrip us completely. But that is not a question that is considered in this text. Rather, we will stick with the (apparently) simpler question as to whether big data approaches can even match the results of the typical human analyst. We will seek to show that overreliance on big data can actually lead to poorer conclusions than those that can be reached by a typical human analyst. We will seek to demonstrate that there are serious limitations to what can be achieved through the big data approach, and there is good reason to believe there will be a vital role for the human analyst well into the foreseeable future.

A Note About Technology

The issues presented in this book can be contentious. Perhaps, as is the case with many other prickly areas of human discourse, the major problems may be resolved with a clear definition of the terms of the argument. To avoid "talking past one another," it is useful to make some clarifications at the outset. First, please note that it is only the adequacy of using a strict big data approach that is being questioned in this book. The advantages of using the algorithms of statistical learning, per se, are not under fire.

The term *statistical learning*[10] as used here is meant to be synonymous with other terms such as *machine learning*, *automatic learning*, and *computer learning*. Statistical learning is the use of algorithms to make conclusions from data that can provide value for problem analysis. The key elements of this definition are contained in the words *algorithm*, *data*, and *value*. We are talking about mathematical or logical approaches that can be coded into computer algorithms and that can provide benefit for any analyses that can lead to results that are of interest to human beings.

Oftentimes, the application of statistical learning techniques can lead to the construction of mathematical models that can be used for prediction, classification, or simplification purposes. It is not required that the statistical learning algorithm be totally self-sufficient; it merely needs to add value to the analysis at hand. This definition is constructed to be wide enough to include supervised and unsupervised analysis of all types. Some current examples of statistical learning algorithms include neural networks, classification trees, nearest neighbor clustering, and support vector machines, along with the wide variety of more traditional statistical methods. We agree, wholeheartedly, that these methods can be quite effective and should be considered as useful elements of the analytical toolbox.

The use of such tools is not considered to be the principal problem with the big data approach. Rather, the fundamental question that is addressed here is whether the use of any such algorithm on sufficiently large sets of observational data can be expected to produce results that are equivalent to what can be done with the assistance of the human analyst. By human analyst, we mean an entity that provides additional knowledge to the problem under study. This knowledge could come in the form of judgement, aesthetic evaluation, or historical context for the problem at hand, in addition to factual information. (In the most general view, such an analyst need not be strictly human, but it will be assumed in this book that for the majority of cases it is a human intelligence that ultimately serves in this function.) We will refer to this functionality as a human analyst throughout the rest of this book. The issues that will be discussed depend on features of the data that can, in general, lead to difficulties regardless of which statistical learning algorithm is being employed. The argument that is presented here focuses narrowly on the potential problems that can arise from an overdependence on the size and complexity of large data sets to overcome any analysis issues.

Navigating Big Data

A useful analogy can be drawn between the problem posed by big data and the use of road navigation systems. For many situations, the advice given by these systems can be quite helpful to a driver trying to negotiate the complexities of our road systems. But, as many of us are aware, problems can arise if our reliance on these systems is blind. One such incident is the story of how multiple drivers were directed to take a shortcut to the Denver airport that instead got them all stuck in the mud on an inaccessible secondary route.[11] Another case involves a driver who was led by his routing application to turn onto a flight of stairs. In still another example of potential disaster, a driver was led up a steep road almost to the point of tumbling off a 100-foot cliff.[12] Although routing algorithms may work perfectly thousands of times, there are still some situations in which the context can be critical. It is this same fundamental problem, as it can occur in more general data analysis situations, that will be explored in detail in the rest of this book.

This book targets the quality systems analyst, and we will assume expert knowledge that is embodied by the human analyst is similar to that possessed by the typical quality practitioner. The type of statistical learning algorithms that might be employed are those that would be available to these same generic practitioners. Finally, the data that are available for analysis also resemble those that are available in a typical quality analysis situation. We seek to understand the real-world problems that can occur if one embraces the assumption that big data is all that is necessary to produce a proper analysis. We also seek to demonstrate that these potential problems can be addressed by proper human intervention. It can be essential to consider the conditions of data collection to provide meaningful analyses; without thoughtful analysis, these data problems can lead us astray, despite the quantity of data at hand.

Structure of This Book

The structure of the book is meant to be as straightforward as possible. First, we will assess the scope of the possible problems that can occur in the big data approach. Second, we will provide detailed numerical examples of each type of problem that can occur. Finally, we will demonstrate that statistical approaches exist that can be used to correct or reduce the impacts of the various problems. In general, these "fixes" are not something that can be found through a search of the data themselves, regardless of how big the data set is. Indeed, many of these challenges can be exacerbated by increasing the data-set size and complexity. Rather, it is the timely interjection of context expertise that is the crucial ingredient.

The overall objective of the book is to alert quality practitioners to the potential problems of depending on a big data-only approach to guide their analysis and to demonstrate they play an essential role in providing the additional knowledge necessary to achieve the correct answer. As more data and complex analyses become readily accessible, the lessons in this text are meant to caution the quality practitioner into thinking first before rushing headlong into a big data analysis.

2

Potential Data Problems and How They Arise

There are many ways problems can occur when collecting data in today's world of quality and process analysis. Errors have been a feature of data throughout history, but the unprecedented increase in data-set sizes seems to have more importance than ever when dealing with these errors effectively. As more data are collected in increasingly diverse ways, it is almost inevitable that some data will become compromised. *Compromised* means the data are deficient in some way, through unintended omissions, additions, or modifications. This expectation seems to remain true, even though the collection devices involved in the system are becoming more reliable all the time.

The ability to grab, collect, and analyze a wide variety of new data types can lead to an increase in the number of potential problems as well. To understand how these data problems can lead to analysis issues, we must first examine how such data sets are generated. Although each individual installation will be unique, there are likely to be some broad generalities that should be typical for most applications. Data may come from four sources:

1. Real-time in-line process data

2. Off-line testing data

3. Historical data

4. Expert opinion data

Each of these data types has its own unique characteristics and tends to be associated with particular types of data issues. Real-time data, for example, often are gathered through in-line automatic data collection systems. These data collection systems can employ a broad variety of sensors, which are embedded in the control and monitoring systems associated with a manufacturing process. Each sensor can produce a stream of measurements of the process on a near continuous basis.[13] Before taking a deeper dive into the four data sources, consider a couple of concerns in data collection: rapid collection and formats.

Rapid Data Collection Concerns

Some sensors are so fast in their acquisition times that it is possible to sample hundreds or even thousands of points in a relatively short time period. In most industries, such real-time data acquisition systems are becoming commonplace, with more of them being installed every day. For most quality analysts, access to rapidly collected process data can become a mixed blessing. On the positive side, there is the increased potential for providing more data that are pertinent to solving a process problem or for characterizing performance. On the negative side, however, it may require a lot of data sifting and manipulation to ensure the most appropriate data are used.

Sometimes, the data access might become more limited as acquisitions grow larger. Restrictions can occur when the amount of raw data is too great to be saved for any significant length of time due to storage limitations, resulting in the dropping of data. Even though storage cost is decreasing all the time, it is unusual for data measurements to be recorded without limitation. For example, it is quite popular to overwrite the old data with new data on some regular and recurring basis to save storage space. Other attempts to alleviate some of the issues with storage sizes can force users to resort to the summary data instead of individual data points. Using summary information can be useful for production reports and management surveys but often does not provide the critical level of detail necessary for quality investigations.

Another problem that occurs regularly in current applications is that databases tend to be static in nature. In other words, once their design is established, it is difficult to add or delete data elements. For data collection where the process is dynamic and ever-changing, this type of collection can lead to a mismatch between what is collected and what is useful for solving problems. In the worst cases, this disconnectedness may lead to the formation of chunks of data—somewhat like islands in an archipelago—that must be bridged to support a proper analysis. If the collection system is is not integrated, then the different subsets of data may not have compatible formats.*

Format Concerns

When various formats are used for different data subsets, integration may be difficult—even impossible—to accomplish. How difficult depends on the details of how the sources differ, which can be, in some situations, quite severe. Too often, practitioners must devote tremendous resources and time to constructing a single data set that is an amalgam of several smaller data sets. Because achieving this consolidation presents difficulties, the finalized data set that is available to the practitioner is often a compromised data set that may suffer from such weaknesses as:

1. Missing cells

2. Duplicate or nearly duplicate variables

3. Data at different time scales and intervals

4. Data that are convenient to collect rather than directly useful

5. Unequal sample sizes (large amounts of unimportant data mixed with small amounts of interesting data)

For instance, you could be faced with the challenge of correctly analyzing two separate data sets that might look like the examples presented in Tables 2.1 and 2.2 on page 12. Notice that some of the variables overlap between the data sets, which is not true of all of them. Even when the same variable names appear in more than one data set, the analyst should check to make sure the same names refer to the same physical measurements. Often, subtle differences in the data definitions can cause real problems for the analyst if he or she is unaware of these potential problems. Even when the definitions appear to be equivalent, there could be subtle operational differences that might influence the final analysis. Oftentimes, the most difficult issues arise because people assume, incorrectly, they know exactly what the variables mean.

---

* A good example is shown in the following article: Thomas Vollmer and Robert Schmitt, "Integrated shop floor data management for increasing energy and resource efficiency in manufacturing," 2015, accessed May 3, 2021, https://www.researchgate.net/publication/280696598_Integrated_shop_floor_data_management_for_increasing_energy_and_resource_efficiency_in_manufacturing.

Table 2.1 Example A of a realistic data set.

Machine	Operator	Temp.	Pressure	Step 1 duration (seconds)	Step 2 duration (seconds)	Length (m)	Time of measurement (hours/mins/sec)
C4	2010	405 °F	1.2	4.7	12.3	32	11:01:12:43
Cfour	2010	407 °F	1.1	4.8	12.5	32	11:01:13:45
D6	2010	403 °F	1.0	4.7	12.6	33	11:01:14:52
D6	2100	402 °F	1.0	4.6	12.6	32	11:01:16:03

Table 2.2 Example B of a realistic data set.

Process number	Operator	On time?	Visual rating	Machine post	Testing protocol	Length (m)	Time of measurement
C4	IJ4	Yes	3.0	IJA	Old	2.12	11:04:00
C4	IJ5	Yes	6.0	IJB	Old	2.15	11:14:00
D6	IJ6	Yes	2.5	IJC	Old	2.70	16:00.00
D6	IJ7	No	7.0	IJD	New	2.54	11:24:00

Off-line Testing Data

In addition to the extensive sets of real-time data that might be collected, supplemental data from off-line processes can also support the real-time process. For example, you may test various samples obtained from the overall production process at a specified sampling rate. These items may be tested either on the spot or in a separate location such as a laboratory. Usually, the application of such off-line tests is performed at a slower pace than production, and you can experience significant time delays between the two. The sampling plans employed to collect these test samples can also be important. Sometimes, the test samples are selected randomly from the process, but there can also be more systematic collection protocols such as "first in the run" or "only at production shift changes," etc. It may even be possible that only suspect samples are extracted from the normal production stream for further inspection. All these options that are used in the sampling of test data can influence the way the data should be analyzed.

It is rare that these samples will be collected in a way that would satisfy a strict statistical definition of representativeness. A great deal of collected data turn out to be the result of taking a convenience sample, since avoiding process interruptions and scrap material can be paramount. It is rare to test samples that describe the entire process in detail. The bare minimum that is usually required to make these data useful for quality analysis purposes is to track a particular product order or identify the specific type of machinery used in creating the sample.

Sometimes, it may be impossible to link a particular point of the process flow to an individual laboratory sample. The testing process data produced usually come from specialized laboratory equipment that is running pre-established testing protocols. The final data generated from this process may take from minutes to days, depending on the difficulty of the lab tests. Often these laboratory data tend to get stored for longer periods of time than production data, which could also mean that test results might be stored in separate data sets.

Different models of testing machines may also have differing data characteristics that need to be considered when combining data for an analysis. It can be helpful to think of the testing process as being like the in-line monitoring process. Testing is an additional sampling of the process that is also made with sensors (usually of a more sophisticated nature) at a different sampling rate. Table 2.3 shows an abbreviated example of a laboratory data set.

Table 2.3 Example of a laboratory data set.

Item number	Tester	Elasticity sample 1 (MPa)	Elasticity sample 2 (MPa)	Breaking point 1 (MPa)	Breaking point 2 (MPa)	Length (cm)	Time of measurement (hours/mins/sec)
10000	Joseph	3.2	3.6	105	102	40.01	11:01:12:43
11000	Joseph	3.3	3.8	101	103	40.05	11:01:22:12
12000	Junipera	3.5	3.6	104	105	40.10	11:02:02:03
13000	Junipera	5.2	5.7	98	92	51.21	11:02:10:15

The off-line testing data can have similar deficiencies to those that may occur in the data collected from in-line systems, including missing data and poor sampling design; however, there are some additional challenges that are somewhat unique to testing data.

One of the new problems that can arise stems from the way laboratories tend to handle outliers. An *outlier*, statistically, is an observation from a different distribution than the one of interest. The trouble with this definition is that it can take a large amount of data to ensure the observations under question are truly representative of anticipated distributions. Often, lab procedures are sensitive to the preparation of materials, setup conditions, and environmental conditions, which can result in creating unusual values occasionally.

Many testing procedures anticipate this problem by establishing preset procedures to detect and remove potential outliers. A common approach is to discard the highest and lowest values automatically and then use only the remaining data points for calculations. Another popular procedure is to condition that removal of values on precomputed tolerance limits that are, perhaps, based on intra-laboratory testing results. In either case, application of these approaches can alter the statistical data properties, which can then lead to compromised final results. If the data point that is being eliminated is not an outlier but merely a rare instance from the assumed distribution, then the data can be biased as a result.

Another unique problem that can occur with testing data derives from the fact that many of the tests are destructive. A destructive test, by definition, destroys any possibility of obtaining further results on that particular sample material once it is tested. The destructive nature of many laboratory tests can lead to at least two additional concerns:

1. Methods of dividing the test materials into subsamples

2. The possibility of mixed modes of failure

Whenever these kinds of data are made available to an analyst, great precaution should be taken to ensure any analysis performed adopts a consistent approach. Clearly, it can be difficult to ascertain whether data are correct simply through a cursory examination of the data on their own. Cases such as these will lead to perfect examples of the importance of the analyst's knowledge of the investigation to a successful conclusion.

Historical Data

Integrating historical data with timelier information that is available from real-time systems can prove useful. Historical data could be taken from older production and test results, but it could also be taken from specifications or process notes entered by in-line personnel or special observers. In some cases, these supplemental data could originate from the equipment manufacturers, suppliers, or other external sources. Most of the time these data sets will be difficult to merge directly with the data that are collected using procedures that are operating according to detailed in-house requirements. There are cases where supplemental data might also be limited to summaries or to a list of extreme cases only. There are circumstances in which collecting the data has little to do with productivity or quality issues, and has everything to do with support for legal or auditing reasons. Since the sources of historical data are usually more diverse than typical sources of data, there might be several versions of historical data that are simultaneously kept in separate departments. Once again, these multiple viewpoints might lead to problems in combining the data in meaningful ways, which can be a huge challenge to the analyst attempting to create a useful data set for analysis purposes.

Expert Opinion

Finally, the quality analyst might have access to process and product experts who can supplement the objective data with their personal observations or ideas. Such expert opinion, as it is called, may come from operators, maintenance personnel, engineers, scientists, managers, or others. Often, supplemental information is in the form of process logs or even stories recounted from disconnected observations of the process. Sometimes, expert opinion can be anecdotal in nature, with cases selectively dredged from the individual's idiosyncratic experience. It is possible that expert opinion can be theory-based as well. Someone's experience or training might lead the individual to develop personal theories about the behavior of the process under study that can provide useful insight for the analysis. For all these reasons, expert opinion data can often be the most difficult to integrate with the other formats.

A hidden challenge of expert opinion data is that it is often presented as textual, rather than numerical, entries. Although there are methods that have been developed in text mining to convert some of this expert opinion into quantitative results, often the practitioner is forced to use input more informally. In many circumstances, this expert opinion is used only when one is trying to interpret the results of analysis rather than it being integrated as an essential component. Ideally, this information should be directly incorporated into the main thrust of the analysis rather than being restricted to a secondary role. Table 2.4 shows an example of an expert-opinion data set.

Table 2.4 Example of a data set based on expert opinion.

Process number	Expert	Date	Comments
H25a	TS	11–May	Underset height control 1 unit
H25a	TS	12–May	Weight calibration too low by 1 percent
H26	JJ	1–Aug	Humidity over 80% causes excess sticking
W20	KR	2–Aug	See special stay linking foot pedal pressure and engagement
W20	JJ	10–Aug	Added new cases to kw study
X10	PD	10–Aug	Vendor 12 concentration needs recheck
X10	PD	11–Aug	Vendor 12 now requalified

It might also be appropriate to mention non-numerical data analysis since using it is becoming more common in modern analysis efforts. Such data can come in various forms such as photographs, sound recordings, network designs, enzyme shapes, and others.

As discussed in Chapter 1, the varieties of this data can be astounding. Although there may be a few methodologies that use this type of data without modification, it is safe to say that nearly all quantitative analyses of such data are based on first abstracting features from them. These features, either because they are numerical or because they can be counted, constitute the actual data for analysis in nearly every case. For example, in facial recognition, a photograph is often scanned for the presence of predefined features (such as face width or eye-to-eye distance). Some of these features may be actual measurements, while others (for example, eye color) might merely record the presence or absence of a feature. So, a particular set of photos could be reduced to a collection of numeric features and the frequencies of another set of presence/absence features.

The number of such secondary derived variables will depend on the application, but it is limited only by the researcher's creativity. For most realistic big data applications, expect at least 20 to 30 such features, but the list can be substantially larger in a novel situation in which the analyst is still searching for possible models. In any case, these values are then used to represent the information that is contained in the picture (or other non-numeric data) in whatever analysis is planned.

Pictures may be inherently richer in information than numbers, but usually that information must be translated into numerical features to feed the actual analysis. When the original data are an interview or an open-text reply, it can be necessary to allow a human expert to transform the conversion to numerical data. That is, the human expert must interpret and recodify the original content into concepts that are useful for the analyst before the full analysis can proceed. Think of all the uploaded videos that are available on the Internet, which helps us understand that this type of data is an important part of modern data analytics. Indeed, it is often assumed that in the future, most data will originally be in some kind of non-numeric format from which numeric data must be extracted. The fact that there is normally an unlimited number of features that can be extracted from a given photograph or recording immediately lends itself well to the idea that more data are better.

A key takeaway is that the majority of non-numeric data are first converted to numerical data (at least to the point of being scaled, ranked, or counted) before being used in the quality analysis. Therefore, all the issues that have been discussed regarding inherently numeric data can also affect the analysis of these other types of big data. In the same way, the details discussed in the remainder of this book can be valuable for all categories of data.

HACCP Applications

Another common case for the use of big data comes from the need to track product development histories and environments such as in hazard analysis critical control point (HACCP) applications. The need to collect all the data for later use can arise in many activities that are required or statutory in nature. The scope of these applications can lead to even greater risk of problems identified earlier in this book. The analyses based on these data become even more problematic, and the practitioner is forewarned to take appropriate measures. In many cases, for these situations, the inclusion of expert opinion can be crucial.

Substituting big data for reasoned analysis is improper use of information that can lead to disaster. The size of the disaster's impact will depend on the nature of the application. Any decision made based on a faulty analysis can lead the user to make costly mistakes in application in the right circumstances. Sometimes the impact of a poor analysis can manifest itself in extra scrap or wasted resources only, but it can be much worse. It is easy to imagine situations in which an improper big data analysis can lead to lost sales or insupportable warranty claims. From a societal standpoint, it is also possible to bias whole systems against individuals or groups[14] because the analyst did not adapt the analysis for the kinds of mistakes outlined in this book, which can be another example of how incorporation of local expertise can alleviate potential problems. Some of the later chapters that deal with the impacts of missing data and the need for randomness can be especially important in this regard. Thoughtful application of the "fixes" presented in this book can help alleviate the impacts of these issues.

The Problem of Modified Data

While the purpose here is not intended to address the problems with intentional "doctoring" or the lesser evil of accidental modifications, such problems can occur. In most cases, these types of compromises can be treated as special cases, as noted in examples throughout the book. For example, it might be possible to treat intentional deletion as a type of censoring. Likewise, "cherry picking" data can sometimes be covered as a lack of randomization. But clever manipulation of the data can prove to be a death knell for valid analysis purposes, so all efforts should be made to avoid it and to correct it where possible. For most of the following cases, it will be assumed that the compromised nature of the data is due to the detailed environment of the data collection process rather than any intentional maliciousness.

Prevalence of Data Problems

Just as the types of data difficulties can depend on the particular situations associated with an application, so can the frequencies of problematic occurrences. Although there are not that many articles that deal with estimating the prevalence of data problems in quality applications, there are many that cite these problems as being common and pervasive. Only one of the issues on our list seems to have garnered enough interest to stimulate quantitative studies. This is the problem of missing values in data. An article that tracked missing values in scientific study data shows that 15% to 70% of considered data sets are reported to be impacted by missing values.[15] In my experience, missing values can occupy as much as 20% of the cells in most large data sets. These are data sets that often have dozens of columns in them and thousands of rows. A cursory examination of some online data sets that are available on the web also supports this estimate of the level of missing values. The frequency of the other kinds of problems that are investigated here is not as well documented, but one can assume these issues might occur with similar frequency in practice.

Data Problem Impact

The impact of problem data can also vary with the application details. The potential damage that can be done by compromised data depends not only on the sheer number of such values but also on how critical this information is to the analysis. It is not difficult to induce a large bias in the final analytical results, even with only one or two well-placed missing values. There are biases as high as 300% in some studies due to seemingly minor underlying data problems. Deleting data values and variables without adequate thought can produce problems. Sometimes, the analyst can be fooled into thinking that absence of evidence means evidence of absence, but making this mistake can lead to disaster. Only a thorough examination of the particular data set at hand can establish which problems may occur, but in general, it is safe to assume that some level of occurrence of these problems always exists in practical data sets. If this assumption of some level of compromised data is appropriate, then the techniques for recovery that are covered in this book should always be considered when trying to solve a real problem before resorting to more automatic methods, such as those employed in big data methodology.

Scoping the Issues
Instead of All the Problems

Clearly, there are lots of challenging issues that arise when dealing with the different types of realistic data that may be available to the quality practitioner. Each particular data set will have its own peculiarities that depend on the details of the application. An experienced analyst will almost certainly have gained enough understanding of the production and data collection processes to help him or her anticipate potential problems and adopt improved approaches. Because it is difficult to anticipate the diverse issues readers may encounter, we will resort to examining the problems in a more general light, without presupposing any specialist knowledge.

We will deal with the essential issues that can be associated with the analysis of any set of data when viewed from a statistical knowledge perspective. In a similar vein, the solutions to the problems that are discussed here will concentrate on demonstrating sound, general approaches that should be applicable in almost any situation, rather than one-off cases that might occur. The hope is that the quality analysts reading this text will be able to blend these approaches into their standard routines to correct and enhance their results.

3

Designed Experiments Versus Big Data Analysis

One of the biggest attractions of using big data is the promise that one might be able to extract valuable information from data that are collected without special effort—or for unrelated reasons. In this case, the data that serve as fodder for the big data technology could consist, primarily, of observational data. Observational data are produced as a normal part of the operation of a system or process without consideration for their potential use in analysis. In the case of a manufacturing system, this kind of data usually would be obtained when the process settings are controlled to levels that are thought to be optimal for good performance in terms of the quantity and quality of the product.

Although there may be a few times when process excursions get included in these types of production data sets, it would be unusual for there to be much extreme data in any database that are collected in this manner. A company whose production processes always run poorly would likely not last long. Sometimes, it might be the case that these unusual data are considered as being so unrepresentative of the true process performance that they may be excised automatically. In either case, the "vanilla-flavored" data should be predominant for most big data-based analyses. Reliance on stable, well-performing data can have potentially negative consequences for any analysis that is based on it.

Statistically Designed Experiments

A historically successful alternative to using the big data approach to explore a process is to conduct a series of statistically designed experiments.[16] Typically, such experiments are implemented in a series of steps that are recommended to ensure best performance of this approach.

The first step requires a thorough examination of the factors that are most likely to be important to the aspect of process performance that is under study. Based on the opinions of the people who are conducting the experiment, as many of these important factors as are deemed feasible are studied through a *screening experiment*. A screening experiment is a recipe that can be used to specify combinations of conditions that enable the experimenter to use a single study to gain a valuable characterization of the relationship of process outputs to the studied factors. It is quite common in such an approach to have seven factors (A-G), or even more, involved in a single screening statistical experiment.

Although there is no technical restriction that demands it, it is common, for the sake of efficiency, to exercise each of the factors at two possible settings during the test. One of the special properties of the recipes that are available for statistically designed experiments is the fact that unbiased separation of effects can be achieved, even though multiple factors are changed simultaneously. Another advantage that is afforded by statistically designed experiments is the management of the experimental noise that can come from the effects of unexplored factors. Table 3.1 shows the pattern of such a statistically designed experiment. Notice the balancing of effects that is evident in the pattern of changes that are used. Sometimes it can be difficult to achieve the control that is necessary to manage all these required changes, but the effort can reap great benefits.

Table 3.1 Example of a statistically designed experimental array.

Trial	Speed dial setting	Temp	Pressure dial setting
1	1x	100 °F	Low
2	1x	100 °F	High
3	1x	150 °F	Low
4	1x	150 °F	High
5	2x	100 °F	Low
6	2x	100 °F	High
7	2x	150 °F	Low
8	2x	150 °F	High

Chances of Observing Extreme Settings

The usual advice that is given for choosing the specific values for each factor setting is to make them as distinct as possible in their effects on the process. In most cases, distinct implies that one seeks to make the two settings as far apart as possible. The rationale behind this prescription is based on the desire to make the statistical tests that are used in the analysis of the experimental design achieve high power. Power, in the case of a statistical analysis, means the ability to clearly separate and estimate effect sizes. This purposeful attempt to make the data combinations produce large effect differences can mean that the analysis of a statistically designed experiment can be quite different from that employed in big data analysis.

To demonstrate how much of a difference there can be, consider a quantitative example. In this example, we will assume there is a single factor to be explored and that its possible effects can be approximated by a normal distribution. Under these assumptions, we could define an extreme setting as one that is two or more standard deviations from the respective mean of its baseline distribution. Values that are this distance from the mean have a rough probability of approximately 0.025 of appearing in a randomly collected data set. Figure 3.1 illustrates the probability of these extreme settings.

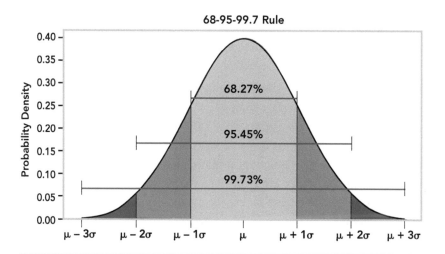

Figure 3.1 Standard normal distribution.[17]

In stark contrast to the observationally collected data that lie behind the big data approach, the statistically designed experiment forces the two settings for the factor to reach these extremes, even when the number of total runs is very small. If the probability of choosing one of these rare extremes is 0.025, the probability of seeing both of these extreme conditions in a randomly collected set of observational data is around 0.025*0.025 = 0.000625, or less than one in 1,000. Such a small probability means the analyst can expect to collect approximately 1,000 observational data points to see the two chosen extreme values appear in the data set by chance only. Although small, it is still well within the range of possibility for large data sets. Thus, if the experiment were focused on a single process variable at a few settings, then it is reasonable to expect that randomly collected data will also contain the kind of event that the statistically designed experiment guarantees will be there.

But even 1,000 observations may not be enough to guarantee the capture of these extreme settings for other reasonable circumstances. Notice that if the occurrence is random and not forced, then no amount of data, no matter how large, can guarantee with 100% chance that these extreme conditions will have to occur in the collected data. At best, the analyst can try achieving a certain probability of observing any set of extreme values. Again, just to emphasize, the designed experiment does achieve a 100% guarantee that these extreme values will appear by its very nature. For the big data approach, you would have to aim higher than 1,000 observations to try to ensure that randomly collected data will see the same extreme settings.

For instance, to have a 99% probability of observing these two extreme settings at random, you would need to collect closer to 5,000 observations rather than the previously estimated 1,000 observations. This sample size is probably still feasible for most applications, but not necessarily all of them. If you change the assumption that extremes are defined as plus or minus two standard deviations to the new criteria of plus or minus three standard deviations from the mean, then the task becomes more difficult for a big data approach. A random collection of data based on this new, stricter criterion would take closer to one million observations to assure success. The requirement for so many observations can severely limit the ability of big data to match the information in a screening experiment.

Big Data Limitations

The study of a single variable in the context of a statistically designed experiment is quite difficult—potentially impossible—through the big data approach alone. But the challenge that is posed to big data by statistically designed experiments is even greater than this. The previous calculations of a required sample size were only for the situation of a single factor whose levels are being chosen at random, which is not a common situation for a statistically designed experiment. It is much more common, perhaps even expected, that a typical screening experiment will study multiple factors at the same time.

An increase in factors makes a huge difference in the calculations. For instance, it is possible for there to be seven factors in a small experiment of only eight total runs. Rather than the chance of observing extreme conditions for a single factor, the analyst now must calculate the chance of seeing 14 extreme settings (two for each of the factors A–G) under random generation of results. Even at the original definition of extreme as being plus or minus two standard deviations from the mean, this new calculation results in a probability of occurrence of such a set of extreme conditions that is on the order of $0.025^{14} = 3.7 \times 10^{-23}$. The reciprocal of this extremely small value is 26×10^{21} observations, which implies that the big data repository would have to be impossibly large to ensure it will capture the same set of test conditions that are automatically contained in the statistically designed experiment data set. This huge number is much bigger than even the largest of today's big data sets and is probably physically impossible to obtain any time soon. So some of the advantages afforded by a statistically designed experiment may be impossible to replace with a random collection of data points.

Costs of Experimentation

Another way to understand the size of the barriers that may arise from a myopic dependence on big data is to consider the economic difficulties that can result from taking that approach. One of the main reasons people are attracted to the notion that observational data can be sufficient unto themselves is the fact that observational data are relatively inexpensive to collect. They are assumed to be a cheap source of information that nearly every analyst and manager hopes to exploit for the purpose of analysis. The dream is a very potent one. If you could derive valuable information from such easy-to-collect data, then they would surely be used continuously in the quality management arena. Of course, inexpensive does not mean zero cost, as there is always some cost involved in collecting data. For our purposes, the real issue is the relative cost of collecting traditional experimental data to that of collecting observational data.

For example, if the cost of collecting a single point of observational data is one cent and that of gaining one experimental point is one dollar, then one could argue that 100 observational points is equivalent to one of the more carefully collected data points based on a cost comparison. Again, this apparent advantage of using observational data lends support to the big data approach. The primary factor that determines this cost differential lies with the level of control that must be exerted during the collection process. If you rely on the process itself to generate observations, that is, observational data, then there should be less cost involved than just inducing changes in the process. Of course, you might have to collect many inexpensive data points to equal the information that is offered by each expensive one. As we have seen previously, the observational approach might need thousands, millions, or even trillions of data points to match the information of a statistically designed experiment. From an economic viewpoint, if the relative cost is 1 to 100, then you might need to spend hundreds, thousands, or billions of dollars in collecting adequate observational data to match what is obtained through the more deliberate designed experiment approach.

Time Issues

The failure of randomly collected data to mimic the results of a statistically designed experiment can lead to other time management problems. A designed experiment usually is an imposition on a production process that can produce interruptions, which means the time required for each run of the experimental array is larger than what you can expect for normal running conditions. So, again, the ratio of these time delays can be important. Often it can take several hours or even days to run through all the experimental conditions that are specified, but this will naturally depend on process details.

If one applies the big data approach and waits for the process to generate the data, it can require a bunch of data to match the information provided by a designed experiment. This could easily run into the millions (or more) for a seven-factor experiment. Thus, a process in which an observation is available every second could end up taking millions of seconds to capture sufficient data amounts. Thus, the need to collect a million such data points to achieve extreme values would take millions of seconds, which is close to a year of production time. This could impose a very leisurely pace to solving problems on a practitioner. In most cases, this observational approach would require more time to accomplish than the more aggressive approach through statistically designed experiments.

Coverage of
Typical Conditions

Further problems can be encountered if one chooses to rely solely on an observational-dependent big data approach. Statistical learning algorithms usually judge the performance of their models by counting the fraction of cases that can be predicted correctly. When most of the data that are used to determine this performance are collected under less-than-extreme conditions, as would be expected from collecting observational data on an active process, then it is likely that the best models will only predict behavior when the process performance is unexceptional.

Consider an example that is somewhat related to the examples given previously. Assume that each data point behaves as if it were drawn from a normal distribution. It is reasonable to assume that around 95% of the values used in the analysis will be found in the middle of the conditions, within two standard deviations of the mean, implying that the models selected as the best by the big data analysis criteria will be those that predict this inner set of values well. Thus, it will be less important to gauge performance on the outer 5% of the data. Notice that this problem does not disappear when more data are added to the study. If the same percentage of values is expected to fall within the normal ranges regardless of the sample size, then the inner values will always be dominant. Even gigantic data sets will not be able to correct this problem on their own.

Readers who are familiar with statistical learning methods may argue that these methods can be modified to handle this problem by using a weighted analysis or other more sophisticated methods. While this assertion is possibly true, this decision is not something that can be derived just from the data at hand. You must provide additional information to know that this kind of weighted analysis could be useful or necessary and to specify how it should be approached. Without the injection of this special information into the analysis, it is likely that this kind of tailored analysis will not be part of data-dependent methodology. The fact that big data assumes no framing of the problem is necessary can be its fatal flaw.

Measurement Error

Measurement error can occur with big data approaches, and it is ubiquitous. There is always some quantity of variation that comes from external sources and that, as a result, is not directly relevant to the variables we are interested in analyzing. It is common for the measurement variation to be independent of the value of the process data. In this case, it is the relative size of the measurement error variance compared to the process variance that becomes critical in the search for the detection of real effects. Generally, when using only observational data, the data will tend to occupy a narrower range of the possible values, which will make the measurement error relatively larger than it might otherwise be.

For example, if the size of the measurement error is constant, then shrinking the observational data range in half can make the relative importance of the measurement error double or even quadruple in size. It can make it more difficult for the statistical analysis to produce clear results, since the noise is relatively more damaging. Simply collecting more data will probably not eliminate the problem because the proportion of typical observations in the repository remains the same. Other types of measurement-error relationships can exist, but this would not be the usual assumption made in the big data approach. Such an adjustment would also seem to require the incorporation of new information that must be obtained from the human analyst.

Expert Opinion

Along with these more specific problems that can occur when relying on big data alone, there is also a larger conceptual problem at work. A critical part of the statistically designed experimental approach is the purposeful inclusion of process expertise at many points in the process.

Experts are involved in the choice of factors and levels for each factor, the number of levels, and the assessment of the existence of interactions. Together, this prework requires close interaction between the experts and the designer of the experiment. None of this communication is assumed, or even allowed, to happen when considering a strict big data approach. The assumption is analysis algorithms are sufficient unto themselves to substitute for expert inclusion as part of the normal procedure. Since the chances of achieving exactly the same conditions as are chosen in a typical design experiment are very small, an observational approach will likely end up with a completely different result than one that would be achieved by a group of experts, which is not an accident.

Efficiency of a statistically designed experiment can be attributed to the merging of expert opinion and statistical considerations. It is hard to see how this dynamic process can be replaced by the static one that is normally employed in big data analysis. The only possible way to do this would be to run the big data analysis under all likely assumptions that can be made to isolate the best results. But, considering the wide number of choices and options that are available to even the simplest experiments, such an analysis seems to be a possibility that must remain in the far future. It is this awkward relationship between situational knowledge and the data that can pose a real challenge for the big data approach.

4

The Challenge of
Missing Values

One of the most common problems of realistic data sets that can arise to derail the powerful engines of big data analysis is the occurrence of missing values. In other words, the information that is contained in the data set can be compromised because particular entries (for example, cells in the table) do not contain meaningful values. It is normal to lose data points at any point of the chain that connects the studied process to the stored data. There are many reasons for missing values:

1. Non-reads from sensing equipment

2. Failure to transmit the sensor readings

3. Failure to store the transmitted readings

4. Accidental deletion (lost data)

5. Purposeful deletion (outlier correction)

6. Improper merges of data

7. Gaps in coverage

Whatever the specific reason is for the loss of data, these missing cells can cause big problems for a big-data-oriented analysis. Consider an example that illustrates some of the possible harm that can arise. The example uses a much smaller set of data than what might be encountered in a real big data study but serves for demonstration purposes. These same types of problems will occur in larger data sets as well, as described later in the chapter. This example data set in Table 4.1 contains only three columns (variables) and nine rows (observations).

The dots in Table 4.1 represent missing entries in the appropriate data cells. Other formats that are commonly used to mark missing data entries include blanks, Not a Number (NaN) codes, or other software-specific codings. Sometimes it is also useful to have different types of code to represent different types of missing values. For example, structurally missing data might be marked separately because they represent entries that cannot be physically possible, as opposed to those entries that are lost accidentally. Even with this simple example, we will see the range of challenges that can be raised by missing values for achieving correct analytic results.

Table 4.1 Example of missing values in a data set.

Input 1	Input 2	Output
1	.	9.174849
1	.	.
1	3	6.597085
.	1	10.23144
2	.	8.655324
2	3	.
3	1	9.503146
3	2	8.497726
3	3	7.465075

The Big Data Approach

The key to understanding the full impact of missing values is to imagine how a big data analysis would approach the analysis of this data set. First, assume that the full data table—that is, all the rows and columns—is of interest for the analysis. Otherwise, it is unlikely that these variables and observations would be selected for analysis. Second, assume that a supervised analysis is being considered. Similar problems can occur for unsupervised analysis, but the supervised case is by far the most common in quality analytics. For this example, we will assume there is a single response variable that is located in the third column of the table and is called "output." The first two columns (input 1 and input 2) are assumed to contain independent variables that are potentially related to the single response variable. A typical task would be to explain the values of the output variable as a combination of the two input variables. This is where potential problems with missing values can occur. Nearly all statistical learning algorithms assume that the input data that are presented to them are a complete data set with no missing values. These algorithms are usually structured so only complete rows of data can be used in the calculations. If the program encounters a missing cell in any specific row (either as output or input), then the rest of the cells in that row are excluded from the analysis. This approach is commonly known as using the complete cases only. It is, by far, the standard way to deal with missing entries. Consider Table 4.2, which shows the reduced data set that would occur if this complete case logic is applied to the example information.

Table 4.2   Complete cases abstracted from the original data set.

Input 1	Input 2	Output
1	3	6.597085
3	1	9.503146
3	2	8.497726
3	3	7.465075

Thus, when missing values are present, it is common for only a subset of the initial data to be used in the analysis. Table 4.2 illustrates the subset of data produced by the deletion of five rows from the original total of nine rows in Table 4.1, which leaves just four complete rows remaining for the purposes of analysis. A simple way to gauge the impact of this action is to notice that the original total of six missing cells leads to the loss of 15 data points. The size of the reduction in any specific situation will depend on the size of the array and the pattern of the missing cells within it. The number of suppressed rows cannot exceed the number of missing cells, but the effects of the suppression can be distributed unequally across the different variables. This can be considered a $100*(27-12)/27 = 100*15/27 = 55.6\%$ loss of information when viewed by cells or perhaps a $100*(9-4)/9 = 55.6\%$ loss of information as measured by loss of rows being caused by the initial 22% of missing cells. This example demonstrates that the effect of missing values can be magnified due to the need to provide complete cases for analysis.

Often, the software used to compute the analysis will not even warn the user that this reduction to complete cases has been made. The assumption of the big data approach seems to be that the data sets are so large that the deletion of a small percentage of the rows is not important. Thus, a true big data approach would probably provide an analysis result based on the subset of data, without emphasizing the fact that several rows have been lost. Notice the lost rows are determined entirely by which cells have missing values, meaning the selection of information used in the final analysis is controlled by whatever mechanism caused the missing values.

There are other ways to approach the problem of missing values. Although it may be tempting to first choose useful variables before restricting to complete cases, this may have already been done as part of an automatic variable reduction procedure. In this example, a simpler model using only input 1 could be used, since most of the missing values occur in input 2. If this altered logic is applied to the example, then the usable data set would look like the one that is presented in Table 4.3. It has been assumed that the complete cases will still be extracted from the reduced table (without input 2) to arrive at this result.

Table 4.3 Complete cases using only Input 1.

Input 1	Output
1	9.174849
1	6.597085
2	8.655324
3	9.503146
3	8.497726
3	7.465075

At first glance, this approach looks more promising. Now the loss of rows caused by the missing cells is only $100*(9-6)/9 = 33.3\%$ compared to the original loss of 55.6%. But, if the true relationship depends on both input 1 and input 2, then you could view the loss as being more substantial. Since this strategy has suppressed 12 cells of information, you can view the loss as $100*(27-12)/27 = 55.6\%$, which is equal to the original evaluation of impact. When viewed in this way, this strategy does not do better, unless the assumption that only input 1 is necessary is correct. Of course, if the analyst knew this assumption to be correct in the first place, then there would have been no need to retain input 2 in the data set. In most cases, either approach to the accommodation of missing values can prove to be problematic.

However, it should be clear that retaining too many variables in the data set can lead to even larger losses. If you keep too many spurious variables in the data set, then the potential increase in missing cells can lead to the deletion of even more data when trying to extract only the complete cases. For instance, if the chance of a missing cell is 10% in any variable, then you can compute the chance of losing any row using the binomial distribution. For example, the chance of losing one or more of m columns of data in any row is given by the calculation $(1-(0.9^m)$. For $m = 2$ columns, this means the percentage chance of losing a row is $100*[1-(0.9^2)] = 19\%$, or roughly 19% of the rows could be lost. If you have a data set that contains 10 variables, then the same calculation of $100*[1-(0.9^{10})]$ yields an estimate of 65% lost rows. And, if you go up to 30 variables, then the percent of likely lost rows is 96%.

Notice that these percentages remain the same no matter how large the data set is. For a hypothetical large data set of 100,000 rows, a suppression of 96% of the rows would leave approximately 4,000 rows in the complete case analysis. The real relationship between the occurrence of missing values and the number of variables will be unique to every application, but the big data approach is likely to have more columns because that is one of its premises. If the likelihood of missing entries is consistent, then this could prove to be a losing battle for large data sets.

Evaluating the True Impact

Simply counting the loss of cells is probably not the optimal way to gauge the true impact of missing values. The real issue revolves around the question of whether important information is being suppressed by the need to deal with missing cells. This is a difficult task, since you do not generally know the value of particular variables until they have been analyzed. To evaluate the true size of the loss, you must know the relationships between the variables. Although you cannot know this information in a practical setting, you can argue from a simulation. The idea is to use the simulated case to help select an approach that should provide generically sound results when it is applied to real data. This is the approach we will use to address the problem raised by the presence of missing values for big data.

To demonstrate the harm that can be inflicted by missing values, it is necessary to assume knowledge that one would not normally have in a real application. As a first step, you can simulate an assumed known relationship between input 1, input 2, and the output. This will be the ultimate answer that the analysis will try to uncover. For this example, the assumed relationship is taken to be Output = 10 + 0.5*Input 1 – 1.0*Input 2. Applying this relationship to the set of nine input combination yields Table 4.4.

Table 4.4 Simulated true data values.

Output	Input 1	Input 2
9.5	1	1
8.5	1	2
7.5	1	3
10	2	1
9	2	2
8	2	3
10.5	3	1
9.5	3	2
8.5	3	3

If you were to perform a two-variable linear regression on this data set, then you should reproduce the true relationship without any residual error. It can also be useful, for the sake of assessment, to create another version of the data through the addition of random error to each of the true response values. This new variable will capture the true relationship between the variables but will also mimic the effects of sampling error. Table 4.5 illustrates what such an error-enhanced output data set could look like.

Table 4.5 Simulated true values overlaid with error.

Input 1	Input 2	Full = Output + Error
1	1	9.174849
1	2	7.44388
1	3	6.597085
2	1	10.23144
2	2	8.655324
2	3	7.519613
3	1	9.503146
3	2	8.497726
3	3	7.465075

These two fictitious (from a practical viewpoint) tables of values can be used to compare the impacts of the different missing value adjustment approaches. To make this comparison easier, Table 4.6 shows the various versions of the data side by side. The "true" column contains the true relationship-based values without error, "full" contains the true values plus random error, "3Vmiss" contains the remaining data based on removing missing values using all three variables, and "2Vmiss" contains the data based on removing missing values omitting input 2.

Table 4.6 Comparing true values to the other results.

Input 1	Input 2	True	Full	3Vmiss	2Vmiss
1	1	9.5	9.174849	.	9.174849
1	2	8.5	7.44388	.	7.44388
1	3	7.5	6.597085	6.597085	6.597085
2	1	10	10.23144	.	.
2	2	9	8.655324	.	.
2	3	8	7.519613	.	7.519613
3	1	10.5	9.503146	9.503146	9.503146
3	2	9.5	8.497726	8.497726	8.497726
3	3	8.5	7.465075	7.465075	7.465075

Consider some simple computations using this simulated data that serve to illustrate the potential harm of missing values to an analysis. The averages of the four different response columns are given in Table 4.7.

Table 4.7 Output averages for the various treatment approaches.

True	Full	3Vmiss	2Vmiss
9	8.343127	8.015758	8.028768

Notice the difference from the mean of the true value is much greater for the missing value reduced data (3Vmiss and 2Vmiss) than for the random error-affected data. Since the difference between the true mean and the full mean is due to random error, this larger difference hints that there is more to the story of the missing value impact than just the impact of random sampling. This extra difference could be attributed to a sample-size reduction (caused by the missing value treatment), to a bias (also caused by the missing value treatment), or both. In general, it will be the case that the impact of missing values can be seen in either or both of these two effects: variance increase and/or bias. The size of each of these potential impacts will depend on the details of the mechanism that lies behind the missing value generation.

Types of Missing Values

So far in our simulation, we still have no lost entries. There is an additional step that needs to be applied to the simulated data set to determine where the missing value will appear in the table (the mechanism lying behind the missing values). Again, these data are simulated, and, therefore, it is possible to know the exact missing value mechanism that is in operation, but this will not be the case in real analysis situations. This mechanism is supposed to represent a physical or logical mechanism that acts on the data (potential) to result in its loss before it can be observed. For example, entries might be deleted through typographical errors, through malfunctions of the recording equipment, via programming errors, or for a wide variety of other reasons. Since it is impossible to anticipate all the specific details of how these missing values might be generated in all cases, the statisticians who have worked with missing values have developed three broad categories of missing value mechanisms.[18] These mechanisms are:

1. Missing completely at random (MCAR)

2. Missing at random (MAR)

3. Missing not at random (MNAR)

Each of these missing value generation mechanisms is defined in a probabilistic fashion. That is, the actually observed set of missing values that occurs is considered to be just one sample from a set of random, possible outcomes. The specific cells that contain missing values could be different if it were possible to rerun the sampling. You cannot perform such a rerun in a practical setting, however, so it is the mechanism rather than the results that remain consistent between applications. It will be necessary to understand these missing value mechanisms in more detail to understand their potential impact on the analysis, in addition to any corrective actions that might be taken.

The first category of missing values is one in which the probability of a value being missing does not depend on other data, missing or complete, in the data set. For the example, this means there is no dependence of the probability of missingness on the values of input 1, input 2, or output. The mechanism that causes the values to be lost is assumed to be independent of the data that are contained in the data set, or MCAR. An example of such an MCAR situation might be the case in which missing values are a result of typographical errors. In general, the creation of typographical errors will not depend on the values that are being entered. This MCAR case is the simplest of the three possibilities, and it can be dealt with in a number of easy ways, which will be detailed later. Nevertheless, even in this simple case, there are some losses of information that can occur due to the presence of missing values. When the MCAR assumption does not hold, it means the probability of an entry being missing can depend on the sum of the variables in the data set.

There are two other types of missing value generation mechanisms that are not as simple as MCAR cases. In one of these cases, the variables that are involved in any existing dependency are assumed to not have any missing values themselves, known as MAR. This situation presents a more difficult problem than the simpler MCAR situation, but there are some opportunities for improving the analysis if you apply the proper approaches. In the final missing value generator type, the missing value chances depend on variables that can have missing values themselves, known as MNAR. This is the most difficult case to deal with, and it usually requires a detailed understanding of the specific case to make the proper adjustments (see Chapter 7 for a discussion of censoring). The remainder of this chapter will focus on the first two types of mechanisms: MAR and MCAR.

As an initial example, you can start by trying to simulate the MCAR condition. According to this assumption, the probability of an entry being replaced by a missing value identifier does not depend on the values of any other variables. To simulate data that obey this condition, you can create a random variable that is chosen without regard for the data at hand. For example, you might create another random normal variable for each cell in Table 4.8 that follows a normal distribution with a mean of 0 and a standard deviation of 1. Then the occurrence of missing value entries is determined by the values of these extraneous random numbers. Using this approach, you could generate a table that looks like Table 4.8. Note that this is identical to the original example data set, since this was the way in which that data were generated.

Table 4.8   MCAR simulation of missing values.

Input 1	Input 2	Output
1	.	9.174849
1	.	.
1	3	6.597085
.	1	10.23144
2	.	8.655324
2	3	.
3	1	9.503146
3	2	8.497726
3	3	7.465075

In this approach to simulating the generation of missing values, you can control the number of total missing values by a rule based on the extraneously generated random values. For example, the following rule—"If the absolute value of the normal variate is less than 1, then one can erase the data table value and replace it with a missing value symbol"—could be replaced with one that uses a threshold of 1.5 rather than 1, which should have the effect of increasing the number of simulated missing cells. Table 4.9 illustrates using a threshold of 1.5 to determine the missing cells. Note that a different selection of values from this missing value distribution could lead to a different set of missing values in the final data set because the missing value mechanism is assumed to be probabilistic.

Table 4.9 Simulated missing values using a different threshold.

Input 1	Input 2	Output
1	.	9.174849
1	.	.
1	3	6.597085
.	1	10.23144
2	.	8.655324
2	3	.
3	1	9.503146
.	2	8.497726
3	.	.

The second type of missing value mechanism is the MAR category, and it can be used to generate missing values in the example data set in a different manner. In the case of MAR behavior, the probability that particular entries appear as missing values is dependent on observed values of some of the other variables in the data set that can be simulated but not as easily as the case of MCAR generation. For example, you can assume that the probability of missing the output variable is a function of the input 2 variable. As a definite example, you can assume that the probability p of an entry in the output variable being missing is a normal variate with mean = p, sigma = 1, and the probability of being missing is 0.01*Input 2. Applying this relationship to the original complete data yields the following p values and normal variate values (see Table 4.10).

Now you need only apply a threshold to the normal values to determine the cells that will be replaced by missing values. Using a threshold of normal > 0 (positive values) to determine the missing cells will result in the deletion of rows 1, 2, 4, and 7, as shown in Table 4.11.

Table 4.10 Generation of MAR missing values.

Input 1	Input 2	True	Full	p	Normal
1	1	9.5	9.174849	0.01	2.028082
1	2	8.5	7.44388	0.02	1.418073
1	3	7.5	6.597085	0.03	–0.71919
2	1	10	10.23144	0.01	0.966068
2	2	9	8.655324	0.02	–0.20534
2	3	8	7.519613	0.03	–0.55223
3	1	10.5	9.503146	0.01	0.596386
3	2	9.5	8.497726	0.02	–2.02544
3	3	8.5	7.465075	0.03	–1.41092

Table 4.11 Simulated missing values under an MAR generator.

Input 1	Input 2	True	Full	p	Normal
1	3	7.5	6.597085	0.03	–0.71919
2	2	9	8.655324	0.02	–0.20534
2	3	8	7.519613	0.03	–0.55223
3	2	9.5	8.497726	0.02	–2.02544
3	3	8.5	7.465075	0.03	–1.41092

Notice that in this particular case, the MAR approach actually results in less lost data than the MCAR method, and yet the mean of the remaining full values (output) is only 7.74. The difference between 7.74 is further away from the true mean of 9 than any of the previous results. This shows that the impact of the MAR mechanism can greatly exceed that of the MCAR-type data.

In general, theoretical considerations find that analyses of reduced (complete case) MCAR data sets tend to have only dispersion inflation without biases, whereas the other types of generators (MAR and MNAR) can lead to both kinds of problems. With this result in mind, you have the option of treating the MCAR cases without any special considerations since there is no expected bias. It can still be quite damaging to lose a lot of data lines, but at least the results should be accurate. This is not the case for MAR or MNAR situations in which the standard approaches can produce inaccurate answers that, depending on the size of the bias, can be devastating. The trouble is that you must know the details of the missing value generation mechanism to know which treatment is required, and that, generally, is impossible to know for sure. It is especially problematic for big data approaches since they do not have the luxury of any human input to help guide them in this matter.

In the case of MAR, it is clear that the standard reduction of data to isolate the complete cases can be dangerous for obtaining correct results. Fortunately, researchers such as Donald Rubin[19] have developed a methodology that can be applied to overcome most of the potential damage that can be caused by MAR missing values. The method is called multiple statistical imputation, and it works in a two-step procedure. First, you build a model that tries to mimic the hidden MAR mechanism that is part of the defining assumption. The model uses this estimated relationship to create possible imputations (replacement values) for each missing entry. Ideally, each imputation will be similar to a random draw from the distribution that is associated with each variable. Because there are multiple imputations rather than just one, the hope is that the mean and variance of the true distributions will be fairly represented through the combination of the imputed and the complete data. The overall effect of this approach is a reduction in the potential bias in results.

Details of the approach can be found in other references, including Rubin's work.[20] Due to the complexity that is required in this approach, it is best implemented in specifically designed computer code such as the Multiple Imputation by Chained Equations (MICE) procedure in Python.[21] Table 4.12 shows what one of the imputed data sets might look like using MICE.

Table 4.12   Imputed data sets using the Python MICE program.

Input 1	Input 2	Full	Full + miss	Full + imp
1	1	9.174849	.	9.327773
1	2	7.44388	.	8.10301
1	3	6.597085	6.597085	6.597085
2	1	10.23144	.	9.327773
2	2	8.655324	8.655324	8.655324
2	3	7.519613	7.519613	7.519613
3	1	9.503146	.	9.327773
3	2	8.497726	8.497726	8.497726
3	3	7.465075	7.465075	7.465075

The mean of the full + imp column, which contains a mixture of complete cases and imputed values, is now 8.313461, and this is much closer to the mean value of the full data (8.343126) than the mean of the full + miss column, which is 7.746965. Since it is usual to run at least four imputations, it is to be expected that the mean over all 9 x 4 = 36 values (imputed and complete) will even be closer to the true value. This approach can provide a considerable advantage when the missing data are MAR. It should be considered mandatory to apply this imputation approach for fitting complex models to larger data sets with many missing values.

Big Data Processes

As discussed, the existence of missing values can be challenging for a big data approach. Since the analysis is supposed to proceed without the injection of additional human knowledge, there seems to be no way for the big data analysis to proceed, except by assuming that the worst case is always active. Since MNAR approaches are specialized, there is no general treatment that can be applied to them. Even when the big data analyst is content to assume a MAR generator, it could lead to great difficulty for an automatic approach. There is almost no treatment of these issues in current big data analysis, which is probably due to the wrong assumption that these few missing cells do not matter in the face of all the other data at hand. It is likely that current applications can lead to large undiscovered biases.

More Data as a Solution

It is worth considering whether simply gathering more data will automatically make the presence of missing values less troublesome. For the deleted observations to have a reduced effect on the final estimates, they essentially must turn a MAR or MNAR situation into one that more closely resembles a MCAR situation. If this can be achieved, then you are validated in the assumption that there should be little or no bias attached to the estimates. But if the additional data do not overcome this fundamental problem, then the same likely problem with bias could occur. This would seem to be a matter of data coverage rather than sheer quantity of data. If the full range of the relationship between variables is explored in the complete data cases, then it is probably true that the absence of some observations, namely those coming from missing values, should not affect the resulting fit. This coverage depends on the sampling scheme that drives the collection of data. If some areas of the design space are never explored, regardless of the number of complete cases, then you can see that the fits will be subject to difficulties.

Unfortunately, you cannot appreciate what part of the design space is being covered without some knowledge about the context of the analysis, and this is exactly what the big data approach wants to prevent. Even when adequate coverage of the design space is obtained (by accident), the coverage may be uneven. If the missing value generation specifically screens out certain areas of the design space, there still may be resultant biases in the fitted estimates.

Increased data-set sizes are also likely to cause an additional problem due to missing values because it is assumed that big data will collect a wider variety of information. It is likely that the inclusion of more and different variables will lead to more missing values in the data set. We have seen how the addition of columns can increase the number of deleted rows when extracting only the complete cases, which should be exacerbated when there are more variables in the data set. The increase of data-set sizes and complexity may combine to do more harm than good when it comes to the impact of missing values on big data analysis. It is difficult for the strict big data approach to reduce these potential biases successfully, since it would need some infusion of expert opinion about the type of missing value mechanisms as a basis for corrective actions. It is difficult to see how all this necessary guidance could be replaced by a direct interrogation of the data at hand, no matter how large the data set may be. Because of all these issues, it is unlikely that the big data approach by itself can overcome some of the serious challenges posed by the presence of missing values.

The Importance of Identifying Missing Data

As a further comment on the impact of missing values on big data analysis, it is useful to note that some data collection practices can create a dangerous situation from the beginning. As mentioned in Chapter 2, some data collection protocols will purposefully delete data points as they are being considered for inclusion. For example, the system may interpret the missing value as a recording or sensor malfunction and decide to ignore it. This can be a serious mistake. The arbitrary exclusion of data is exactly like the strategy of using only complete cases—only it is worse because the user may have no idea the deletion has occurred. It is basically a hardware version of the software mistake of excising data. Either treatment can lead to the problems we have documented, potentially ending in biased results.

Finally, a comment should also be made on the case in which different types of missing values are coded into the data set. Sometimes, a unique code is used to distinguish the rough cause of the missing entry.

For example, the missing cell can be created by an extraneous mechanism, as detailed in the MCAR, MAR, and MNAR cases previously covered. We have seen how to handle these situations in general through the application of multiple statistical imputation methods. If there are several subtypes of these sorts of missing values, say due to the source subsystem from which they sprang, then the approach may need to be elaborated. That is, the mechanism—and, therefore, the model—that is used in the multiple imputation scheme can be specialized to each type of missing value. To predict "missingness" in variables coming from a sensor, you might use only variables that are causally related to the sensor system. A different set of modeling variables may then be chosen for each of the various missing value types, ultimately resulting in multiple imputation models. Otherwise, the procedure can be similar to what we have seen. One exception to this rule is the case of structural missing values. These are cells that physically cannot be occupied by a valid measurement but are kept for formatting purposes. For example, a pregnant man could have a missing value symbol assigned, but it would not make sense to impute a value for it. The best approach to such instances is to redefine the variables so these placeholders are eliminated, for example, by separating the sex of the respondent and the pregnancy status into two separate variables.

5

The Impact of
Poor Randomization

Big data analysis problems can also arise from the subtle ways data are collected. As detailed in Chapter 2, the ultimate data set that is used for analysis often is a mash-up of several different data sets, each with its own idiosyncrasies and problems.

In a manufacturing setting, these data sets usually consist of measurements that are conducted either periodically on a process or, more commonly, each time a particular process stage is completed. For example, you may record the processing variables attached to a cure cycle or to runs of an extruder. Or, as is seen in more continuous industries, you might do a sampling of process variables every centi-second during some interval of operation. In nonmanufacturing conditions, you can have the same type of issues. Data on an administrative process may be sampled when a project passes a certain milestone or daily through an audit, etc. Examining the sampling plan can help determine what analyses are possible long before the actual values are collected. If procedural or logistical requirements constrain the randomness of the data collection, then that can lead to problems for the big data approach. These problems will not be as evident as missing cells or NaN values sprinkled throughout a data set, but they can cause similar issues with the final analysis.

Randomization and Bias

Let us consider for a moment what randomization is. The Merriam-Webster Dictionary defines a *random variable* as "a variable that is itself a function of the result of a statistical experiment in which each outcome has a definite probability of occurrence." This definition highlights the unpredictability of the data pattern. For the purposes of analysis, this definition can be tightened to something like the entry under random variable, which defines it as "a variable that is itself a function of the result of a statistical experiment in which each outcome has a definite probability of occurrence."

For example, Table 5.1 illustrates 20 data points that will be used to demonstrate the potential problems before scaling it up to what might happen in a big data application. For this example, the distribution is assumed to be a discrete uniform distribution operating on the values from 1 to 9 inclusive. That is, there are exactly nine possible values, and each occurs with equal probability of 1/9. Note that this is not the only feasible distribution that can be used to demonstrate randomness, but it is one that conforms to most people's view of randomness. It is crucial to note that this assumption of the distribution implies an infinite number of possible samples that could be drawn from it either now or sometime in the future. This adoption of a distribution usually implies that any sample, no matter how large it is, will always be a small part of the set of potential values.

Table 5.1 Twenty discrete uniform values.

8	8	9	9
4	1	5	1
9	6	5	8
4	3	1	1
6	3	2	1

The second aspect of randomness beyond the distribution concerns the process that is used in obtaining the sample. As the previous definition states, randomness typically implies independence of sampling from the given distribution as well. *Independence* means that the probability of a particular value being chosen does not depend on the results from any other point that is obtained in the sampling process. Almost always, this independence is taken to be independence in time, as there is usually an order to the collection of individual samples; however, it also applies in cases in which numerous data points can be collected simultaneously. Sometimes in real applications this independence is assured by separating the acts of data collection from data recording so past values cannot bias the procedure. To meet the definition of randomness, the 20 values given in Table 5.1 must be assumed to be independent draws from the specified discrete uniform distribution. Generally, it is this combination of the two criteria, a baseline distribution and independence of samples, that defines randomness. Randomness is essential for most types of statistical analysis and for any analysis that depends on stochasticity.* Its primary importance is ensuring the results of any analysis based on the data are unbiased. Bias is the expected systematic difference between an estimate and its associated true value based on an infinite number of samples. Severe biases can disrupt an analysis to such an extent that results can be substantially wrong.

To understand why bias can be so important, let us look at another example. In this example, the methodology integrity will be determined by the number of correct predictions counted when the procedure is applied to a particular set of data. To be more specific, you might have a set of 100,000 values that is being modeled with a classification tree algorithm.[22]

The algorithm will generate some potential explanatory tree models, say two of them Q and P, whose performance will be compared to determine which is the best model. Although there are numerous other options available for such trees, the best model in this example is assumed to be determined by simply counting the number of correct predictions out of the total of 100,000 that are made by each of the candidate models. We could also perform this evaluation of the models on verification sets, but the moral would prove to be the same. If the point of the modeling were simply to summarize the behavior of the decision tree model on the 100,000 given values, then it could make sense that this simple count might be adequate; however, that is not usually the situation. These 100,000 values are almost always considered as a representative subset of the infinite number of possible values. The best model, by definition, is the model that best predicts the behavior of these unknown values. Depending on the application, these unknowns could be thought as being future observations or contemporaneous neglected ones, but either way they are not part of the data set on which the model is constructed. This change of viewpoint from

---

*Random; involving chance or probability

the data at hand to the potential data can change the criteria for model selection.

This emphasis on potential data is usually handled by the assumption of some theoretical distribution of values and, if some element of stochasticity is involved, it almost demands the use of a probability distribution. This is implied in the very definition of bias that is given previously. Thus, it is the twin requirements of a distribution and independence that are crucial. Notice that adopting the view that one would like to select a model that performs well over an infinite number of potential samples means no finite data set can ever be more than a small fraction of the full situation, no matter how large it might be.

Practical Application

In most applications of statistical learning, whether on big data or not, we test the performance of a given model by comparing its predictions to actual results from a separate data set that has been withheld from the fitting process. These additional data are often called the *verification* or *validation set*. Usually, this verification set is a subset of the original full data, but it can also be resampled data or new data collected expressly for the purpose at hand. In the argument presented here, however these extra data are obtained, it is still a finite sample of the full set of possibilities. In many ways, it can be considered a reduction in the size of the big data since it is smaller than the full data set. Although this procedure usually provides a more robust estimate of the errors, it cannot substitute for the entire probability distribution and, therefore, is subject to the same problems that are discussed here.

The assumption that the data are chosen independently from a discrete uniform random distribution allows you to establish a baseline for doing statistical comparisons. For example, such a uniform distribution should have a mean value that is in the center of the nine values, namely it should be $(9+1)/2 = 5.0$. You can compare the observed sample mean of the collected data to this theoretical expectation to judge how closely the assumptions are matched. For the data contained in the example data set, the observed sample average happens to be 4.7, which is 0.3 too low. If this were a simple figure of merit, then you would need to establish some kind of scale to judge whether this was a small deviation. In the case of a statistical distribution, this scale of judgment is often provided by the standard deviation of the distribution. In the case of the uniform distribution, this standard deviation is expected to be the square root of $[(9–0)^2–1]/12 = 1.6/sqrt(20) = 0.76$, so an observed deviation of 0.3 is small compared to this criterion. Note that this calculation depends on the assumption that the distribution and the independence of sampling are correctly assigned.

There is a potential problem with the big data approach when randomness is required. Remember that generally speaking, no additional information about the data collection is supposed to be used in the analysis besides that which is contained in the data points themselves. So, assumptions about distributions and independence of sampling are not really allowed by the methodology, and yet they can be crucial for the analysis. This leaves big data analysis with the recourse of trying to determine the distribution and independence by examining the data themselves. This, however, is no easy task, and it is considered nearly impossible by many statistical experts.

To understand how difficult it can be to make these judgments from the data alone, consider the selection of a probability distribution. The number of statistical distributions is essentially infinite since a discrete probability distribution is defined by three characteristics:

1. Every considered event has a probability greater than zero.

2. Every unconsidered event has a probability equal to zero.

3. The sum of all the probabilities of the events equals one.

One choice that meets these requirements is the discrete uniform distribution on the values from 1 to 9 that was used to generate the example data. The events consist of the nine numbers from 1 to 9, and each has a probability assumed to be exactly 1/9. The sum of the nine probabilities do indeed total to one as required, but there are many other distributions that are minor variations on this one that can also satisfy the criteria. For example, the true distribution might be one that assigns a slightly higher probability of 1/9 + 0.02 to the value 1 and a slightly lower value of 1/9 − 0.02 to the value 2 while leaving the other probabilities equal to 1/9 as initially specified. The sum of these nine values should still be one since the small discrepancies cancel out, and the criteria of a proper statistical distribution are still met. This can be a nightmare for the big data approach. It will require a great deal of data to tell the difference between these two distribution choices with any sense of certainty. And, if you are fortunate to have enough data to distinguish between the two distributions displayed here, you can always change the discrepancies to make them smaller. For example, you can assign probabilities of $1/9 + 0.00000000001$ and $1/9 - 0.00000000001$ to the values of 1 and 2, respectively. For such a case, it could take billions or trillions of data points to distinguish between the two choices. You might argue that simpler distributions are preferable, but this recommendation depends on you providing additional information to the analysis beyond what is contained in the data alone. You might also want to assume that being close to the correct distribution is good enough, but, once again, this is not really allowed if you must depend entirely on the data for everything. All the various, slightly different choices for a distribution should be equally preferable in a strictly data-driven approach.

Other Challenges

Adherence to the strict requirements big data analysis places on knowing the context of the data can lead to additional challenges. For example, it might be part of the process under study to record only integer values. This restriction to integer values may also be due to rounding or truncation that is encountered during the storage process. Even the fact that the range of numbers is 0 to 9 is likely to be explained by the operational details rather than being something that can be seen from the data. It is fundamentally impossible to know that the values are restricted to this range when you are restricted to the data only to determine the choice of the range of a distribution. There is a possibility that, no matter how large the data set, new observations could be more extreme in one direction or the other.

The challenge becomes even greater when you consider that the discrete uniform distribution is simply one of many potential patterns of probabilities that can be considered valid distributions. Even if you restrict the search to discrete data distributions, you might have a binomial distribution or a hyper-geometric distribution instead of the discrete uniform. Somehow, the big data approach must distinguish between all these choices by using only data analysis. The same kinds of issues occur for continuous distributions, since there are many choices there as well, such as the normal distribution, the Weibull, or the continuous uniform, that need to be considered. In fact, there is no reason to assume the distribution must be one of the "named" ones, since such a restriction would amount to the imposition of expert opinion. As a result of this difficulty, the big data approach cannot easily determine a baseline distribution.

There is also the issue of whether the data are stable enough to allow this kind of detailed distribution fitting, even if it is considered desirable to do so. To achieve a large number of samples, such as what is assumed in big data analysis, it can be necessary to sample very rapidly, to sample over a long time interval, or to combine separate streams of data together. In any of these cases, it is unlikely that the physical system from which the data are collected will remain statistically stable throughout the data collection (statistically stable meaning that the same single distribution will fit exactly for all time periods). Since the big data approach is trying to ascertain the correct distribution by making finer and finer distinctions, it is almost certain that there will be subsets of the data that do not match one another in the choice of distribution. This leaves the data-driven approach with the problem as to how to determine which subsets of data do agree.

Even if you assume that there are intervals of stability, it would take a great deal of searching and testing to decide where the subset boundaries should be drawn. This would probably need to be actualized by dividing the full data set into possible subsets and then testing for the distribution on each subset before comparing among them. You could easily imagine that the original 100,000 data points might have to be broken up into sets of 1,000 to do this check adequately, but it is unclear how to make the division. You could divide by collection time, but this could miss other underlying patterns. Or, you could divide the full data randomly into subsets, but you must still decide many details to achieve this. If you make the subsets too small, then the number of comparisons that are required might soon grow to be unmanageable.

Combinatorics tells us that there are $100000!/1000!*(100000-1000)!$ different ways to select unique subsets of size 1,000 from the original 100,000. This is a number so large that it is practically impossible to achieve. You must seemingly impose other assumptions on the process that cannot be determined from the data alone. On the other hand, leaving the subsets too large will invite the loss of stability again, but not within the subsets. The very precision that is afforded by large data sets can be a curse when trying to determine these kinds of questions from the data alone.

A complicating factor to this big-data-required search for a distribution is the fact that the choice probably depends on the knowledge of the sampling method being applied. Unfortunately, determining patterns turns out to be just as difficult as determining the distribution. It may seem obvious that it will be difficult to guarantee that no discernible pattern will be found in any particular set of data. Nevertheless, from the point of view of the big data approach, these issues must be solved based entirely on the data at hand. This in turn means part of the algorithm must be able to test for various departures from independence.

Many such tests and procedures[23] have been developed and improved over the years, but their application is not always straightforward. Essentially, these methods test for types of nonindependence, rather than being able to prove once and for all that the data are independently selected. There are many ways the data can be dependent, but there is only one way they can be independent. Similar to what was demonstrated with distribution choice, the differences between the two cases can be made so small as to be practically undetectable by the use of data alone. For example, there could be dependence between every consecutive sample with the probability being adjusted up or down depending on where the value is in the sequence. To be more specific, you could imagine a case in which all data points are independent except for every tenth sample point. This kind of simple autocorrelation can be checked with various statistical time-series tests, but most of these tests depend on the assumption of a particular distribution. So, we are faced with the "Catch-22" that we need to assume the distribution to run the independence check.

The same kind of autocorrelation test probably would not pick up on an issue that is more elaborate. For example, there might be a correlation that occurs only between the numbers six and seven after they have appeared 10 times each or some other arbitrarily complex pattern. This pattern is likely to go undetected, no matter how extensive the search process employed by the big data approach is, and there are many other possibilities at least as complicated as this one that should also be checked. Remember that any simplifying assumption would violate the philosophy of a strict big data analysis. It is clear that unless one is presented with outside information, this process could be indeterminate and inconsistent.

Stability

The issue of stability comes into play for the tests of independence as well, as it's unlikely that any real process will be perfectly consistent for extremely long periods of time. The same issues can occur in the practical application of the independence tests, as was seen for choosing a distribution. Different subsets of the data will likely have different patterns, and any attempt to check all possible subsets is practically impossible for even moderately sized data sets. You might be faced with the necessity of using smaller data sets pulled from the initially large one, which cuts against the grain of the big data promise. All this can be made even more challenging by the fact that the two assumptions of independence and distribution type play off one another and, ideally, would have to be made simultaneously.

Let's clarify the difference between the big data approach and the approach that would usually be employed in a more standard statistical analysis that includes the incorporation of information from a process expert. First (and this can be a crucial difference), the expert would specifically and actively try to randomize the data. This step demonstrates one of the biggest differences between the big data approach based on observational data and the more proactive statistical study. Even if the expert cannot physically manipulate the sampling process, he or she may be able to understand it at a level that also guarantees its characteristics.

Second, the expert uses his or her experience and expertise to assume a type of distribution such as a uniform discrete distribution on the digits 0 to 9. This choice could be determined by the fact that the analyst can actively control the sampling methods to force the data to follow a particular distribution; but, more often, the choice is likely made from experience with the system. Once these assumptions are made, then the analyst would apply whatever procedure was most appropriate using these assumptions. Certainly, the analyst can still use the data as a rough check of his or her assumptions, but this is a far cry from trying to choose a proper distribution without any guidance beyond the data at hand.

Now compare the previous procedure to what might be employed in the big data approach. The algorithm must first use the data to search for a proper distribution and check for independence. This set of tests, which we have seen may not be adequate, could still be applied to the entire large data set. Almost any test, when applied to a large set of data, will have so much statistical power to separate fine differences, that it is likely you will find problems with consistency and stability across the entire data set. If this is true, then the algorithm must choose between eliminating data from the analysis or, more likely, fitting models on smaller subsets of data.

There can be problems both with rapidly collected data and with data collected over an extended time period. It is likely that data sets of larger than a few thousand points will exhibit signs of instability. Reducing the amount of data available from the original 100,000 to this smaller size of a thousand or so would certainly cripple what is considered the essential power of the big data methodology. Other approaches, which might depend on choosing from a pre-established list of potential distributions, would require expert opinion to develop. In the same way, any attempt to allow the program to accept approximations would also require additional input from outside the data as to how to accomplish this task.

A Resampling Approach

A big data analysis program might be able to use a resampling approach to generate a distribution without directly facing the challenges that have been described. Resampling[24] simulates the selection of small subsets of data from the original data to generate an ad-hoc distribution. For example, in the case of the discrete uniform distribution, this might consist of resampling individual values from the 20 with replacement to generate simulations of thousands of samplings. Although this approach can provide some advantages, it does not fully address the issues explored in this chapter. It would still take an infinite number of simulated distributions to match the information contained in a statistical distribution. But even ignoring this fact, there are some problems with resampling. Often, this procedure can produce some idiosyncratic distributions. In the original example data set, there were no observed 7s, and thus the simulated samples could not possibly contain any 7s because of this fact. The simulated distributions would look quite unusual with two separated sections divided by zero probability at the 7's slot. It is likely that decisions based on this pseudo-distribution would not match those obtained from future samplings from this discrete uniform probability distribution because a value of 7 should eventually occur.

In a similar way, any anomalies that occur in the data will be frozen into the simulated distributions. Flukes occurring in the small initial samples can be magnified by the resampling process in this way. If the data are truly unstable, then this resampling approach probably will mix all the patterns together, and this could also lead to an inappropriate distribution. For example, the first 100 samples could have a mean of 5, while the second 100 could exhibit a mean of 6. Random subsets like those created by the resampling process will likely lead to averages around 5.5, but this will not match either observed subset. Unfortunately for the big data approach, the features of the pseudo-distribution are likely to grow even more idiosyncratic as the number of sampled points increases. It is possible that this resampling approach could improve the situation for the big data algorithm, but it probably would take expert knowledge to decide on its adequacy and application.

In summary, there are several challenges related to randomization that can be encountered in applying the big data methodology. There is certainly difficulty to be expected in numerically ascertaining the proper distribution and in testing independence that can be simplified using background information and expert opinion. On a practical level, one of the primary advantages of the ideal standard statistical analysis is the ability to proactively force randomization to occur. This active participation of the expert in forcing the assumptions to be correct is a powerful advantage that is often lost in the observational data approach. Active randomization means trying to break any possible hidden connections between the factors of importance in the study with background variables.

The Risk of Losing Data

A big data advocate may argue that you could simply select the subset of data that meets the randomness criteria from the large data set, but this approach almost certainly means the original enormous data sets will be lost. Each application will be different, but it is likely that sufficiently (accidentally) randomized subsets of data will be a small percentage of the full size. It is doubtful that the big data analysis will produce the same results if you are forced to use only 10% of the original data. The search itself could also create logistical difficulties in trying to isolate the sufficiently random subsets. In this case, there is no guarantee that the desirable data points will fall in sequences or clusters, so the search could be made orders of magnitude more difficult. If the data used in the big data analysis are not properly vetted, then it is likely there will be biases between results that are obtained from them and the true behavior on all those potential, future observations. It is also likely that simply collecting more data will continue to exacerbate this fundamental problem rather than alleviate it.

Another challenge that big data analysts can face is trying to select a sufficiently randomized subset from a larger repository. This problem is best demonstrated by the over-randomization that is often applied in a statistically designed experiment (see Chapter 3).

Imagine there are three variables that have been chosen (through expert opinion) to be studied. These three factors are forced to vary between trials according to the array conditions, but the order of the runs is not specified because it is used to ensure the studied factors are randomized with respect to the unstudied factor. That is, the array rows are often rewritten in random order for the actual physical run of each. It is unlikely that the pattern in the studied variables will match that of some unknown but critical process factor. You cannot directly randomize the vast number of possible unknown factors because they are, after all, unknown to the experimenter. Also, the randomization is achieved only between the studied and unstudied factors. The studied factors are balanced among themselves because of the array properties, but the unstudied background factors could be correlated among themselves. To be more definite with this argument, consider the three factors of temperature, pressure, and humidity. The levels of these three factors are run according to the four rows of the appropriate screening array but in a randomized order. Other factors that affect the results can vary as they might normally do. One of these other unknown factors, (for example, age of product), increases linearly through the time (run order). If the array were not randomized, then this underlying pattern might match the (unrandomized) array pattern and cause bias in the result.

Depending on the relative strengths of the underlying factor and the studied factors, this lack of randomization could hide or even reverse the fitted effects. Randomization of any replicate runs is also recommended for the same reason. Notice that there could be a second unknown variable, such as viscosity, that is correlated with age of the product as well. This relationship between background factors is likely not affected by the randomization procedure in this example. Sometimes additional advantages can be secured by running several replicates of each and changing the randomization order between these replicates. The point of this discussion is that it can require active participation to ensure this randomization of factor effects.

Now we can compare this active randomization approach with that being employed by the big data analyst searching through a large database to find sufficiently randomized observations. Two possibilities present themselves. The database might contain all relevant factors that are necessary to explain the studied phenomenon. In the example, this would require all five factors of temperature, pressure, humidity, age of product, and viscosity to be captured. It is unlikely that any database will actually capture all the pertinent variables, but it is as least feasible. In this case, the analyst will look for a subset of the full data that shows no correlation between any of the five (or larger) variables.

Ignoring the problem of how to determine null correlation from the data alone, which could be just as problematic as the determining distribution, is even more difficult. Remember that the effects of the unknown variables (age of material and viscosity) are unknown. The big data analyst does not know which variables of all the possible choices to randomize against. If the big data repository has 20 variables, then the analyst must look for randomness among all 20 variables. Otherwise, some specialized expert input would probably be necessary. It is likely that some variables will look correlated just by chance, and some, such as age of material and viscosity, will be truly correlated. It is numerically likely that only a very small subset of the full data set will look as if it is uncorrelated among all variables. Notice that it is even possible to find pockets of data where the truly correlated background variables look, due to random variations, like they are uncorrelated. This search could end up choosing some very odd combinations if any conditions matched the criteria. It is likely that the big data analysis would be forced to use only a small fraction of the data in this case. Notice also that the situation is likely to be even more dire as the number of variables increases.

6

Expert Opinion

One of the underlying themes of this book is the fact that the incorporation of extra knowledge, not arising directly from the data at hand, can be the key to overcoming many of the challenges faced in the pursuit of proper analysis. Knowledge about the situation or about theoretical expectations can often mean the difference between a successful study and one that leads to incorrect results. In the previous chapters, this outside information was used in a rather informal manner by aiding in the selection of experimental conditions or in the choice of a background distribution. This chapter, however, will demonstrate how to bring this expert knowledge into the analysis process in a more intimate fashion.

The difference between the big data approach and that of a more typical statistical application is even more glaring when you consider the direct combination of expert opinion with data into one seamless analysis. As discussed in Chapter 2, there are often sources of information that come in the form of rules, observations, or physical principles that can lend efficacy to an analysis but that are not in the form of data that can simply be added to what already exists. And yet, there are ways to incorporate this expert opinion into the analysis in a straightforward way, using Bayesian methodology, that can often provide great benefit.

To make this promise more precise, imagine that we possess a large set of data that avoids all the problems that have been introduced to this point. In addition to these data, also imagine that there is a team of experts or repository of expertise that can be used to provide useful supplemental information for the analysis. For example, the experts may know that because of physical principles, there are only certain allowable values for the various parameters of the fitted model. This information may impose a strict constraint that clearly outlaws certain values for these model features, or it may provide more of a probabilistic tendency that can be used as a guideline. The crucial point for this discussion is that this extra information does not come in the form of data points, but it is coded as knowledge. There are many issues surrounding the elicitation of expert opinion for this purpose, but that will not be the focus for the discussion here.[25] Since the purpose of this book is to emphasize the difference between this method and the prototypical big data approach, it will not be necessary to go into all the background details of this aspect. It simply will be assumed throughout this chapter that the expert opinion has already been made ready for assimilation.

As a simple example, consider the set of data in Table 6.1. Note that these values are very similar to those given in the previous chapter in the example about randomization, but now the range of these values runs from 0 to 10 rather than 1 to 9. These data are meant to represent the number of failures in 10 independent trials of a new methodology that is under test. Thus, a 0 represents 10 successes out of 10 trials, and a result of 10 implies 0 successes out of 10 trials. If desired, it would be straightforward to convert this set of data to fractions or percentages to represent the same information. Note that this set of 10 results is the product of $10*10 = 100$ individual tests.

Table 6.1 Example of failure data.

0
0
1
2
0
3
1
1
0
1

We will take the same approach as in previous chapters by demonstrating the challenge on a simple data set before we scale up the argument to big data standards. The task at hand is to use these data to estimate the fraction failing under this candidate process. The usual way to do this analysis is to simply average the results over the 100 total trials. If you complete this calculation, then the estimated fraction failing is 9/100 = 0.09. Notice that the resulting average is not an integer; it is a decimal number ranging from 0 to 1 by 100ths. If there were no additional expert opinions to be considered in this analysis, then this answer of 9% would probably be the end result of the analysis.

The extra information that is available is assumed to come from various sources such as historical experience that has been gained from observation of the process or perhaps from a knowledge of physical constraints that operate within it. It is often the case that the engineering design will determine the possible values that are achieved in performance. If this were not the case, then you could argue that there is little to be gained through any engineering effort. Because of a feature of Bayesian analysis called conjugate distributions, it is relatively easy to merge the expert opinion into the analysis.[26] Assuming that the observed data are described by a binomial distribution, then it is most convenient to express the expert information in the form of a beta distribution. Notice that this step requires the input of expertise, but in the previous form of framing the analysis.

For example, if the experts think the true value of the fraction failing is approximately 0.05 with a tight standard deviation of approximately 0.025, then the parameters (alpha 1 and beta 1) of the beta distribution will be alpha 1 = 4 and beta 1 = 76. In the conjugate case of having a prior distribution being a beta with these parameters and the likelihood being binomial, then you know immediately that posterior distribution is also a beta distribution with parameters alpha 2 = alpha 1+ the number of failures and beta 2 = beta 1+ the number of successes. The posterior distribution summarizes the combined information in the observed data with the information coming from the experts. Numerically, in this case, the results of combining the data with this prior information is a beta distribution with alpha = 13 and beta =167. Such a beta distribution has a mean value of 13/180 = 0.072 that can be used as an estimate of the fraction failing instead of the original 0.09.

This revised estimate can be thought of as a weighted average of the two individual estimates that are derived from expert opinion and from the data separately (0.05 and 0.09, respectively). Intuitively, one can see that the weights of the data and the expert opinion must be similar in the calculation of this weighted average, since the overall estimate of 0.072 is roughly halfway between the two alternate estimates. This rough conclusion of the size of the relative weights in this average can be made more precise by considering the effect of sample size on the standard deviation of the information. Since the original data are binomial with an approximate p of 0.09 and $n = 100$, the calculated standard deviation is 0.029. Since the final estimate is roughly $p = 0.07$ with a standard deviation of 0.01911, you can solve for the sample size n that would give these values, and you will find that this gives $n = 180$ approximately. So, one way to measure the value of the expert opinion is to consider it equivalent to having an additional 80 data points supplementing the 100 observed test results.

The Essential Difference of the Bayesian Approach

The ability to easily incorporate expert opinion into an analysis through the Bayesian approach is quite general, although some situations that do not easily fall into the conjugate distribution category can require numerical solutions. Many software packages include these techniques. Bayesian analysis provides a powerful way of combining observational data and current knowledge to produce updated knowledge, which then can be used in the next iteration of learning. Now that we have an example of how you might incorporate expert opinion directly into the analysis, we can compare the process with the typical naïve big data approach.

It is this example of incorporating expert opinion directly into the analysis that most clearly shows the crucial differences between big data analysis and more standard analyses. To this point in the book, expertise has been used simply to frame the question. The argument is that, without the ability to do this, then big data is permanently at a disadvantage. The use of Bayesian analysis is substantially different from this example. Because of the rough equivalency of the prior information to an additional data set, you can directly compare the requirements of particular sets of knowledge to the amount of data that would be necessary to mimic them.

In the example just given, it was shown that the assumptions of the experts were roughly equivalent to an additional 80 or so observations to be added to the observed 100, but this result can change depending on the details. Perhaps the experts provided an estimate of p being 0.05 but with a smaller standard deviation equal to 0.01. This change of information, when incorporated into the appropriate beta distribution, would now have parameter values that are closer to alpha 1 = 16 and beta 1 = 304. Then the posterior distribution, when the same observed data and the modified prior information are combined, will have a new alpha 2 parameter of 25 and a new beta 2 parameter of 395. The mean of this new beta posterior distribution is 0.06 with a standard deviation of 0.015. Such a result, when converted to an equivalent sample size, estimates the total sample size at 1,055. So roughly, this finer information is worth 955 additional data points. One can easily see that, with precise enough prior information, this equivalent sample size can increase dramatically. This approach can provide an indication of the certainty of your knowledge base.

Lessons from Extreme Priors

Another interesting way to illustrate this effect is to think about the big data approach in its refusal to incorporate the additional knowledge in this Bayesian light, which can be treated with the Bayesian analysis approach in an easy fashion as well. Although the exact methodology of mimicking indifference using noninformative priors is a little more sophisticated than what is shown here, you get a sense for the impact of using the naïve big data approach by assuming a uniform distribution as the prior where the distribution could have values from 0 to 1, and each value would be equally likely within the set. This represents the situation in which our expert knowledge is insufficient to narrow down the range of possible values to any degree whatsoever. It usually represents an extreme case compared to the usual situation.

It so happens that such a uniform distribution is equivalent to a beta distribution with alpha1 = 1 and beta1 = 1. In this case, because of the small values of prior parameters (both = 1), the posterior distribution will have parameters that are dominated by the data, and the incorporation of the expert opinion will add little to the analysis. Imagine the process when there is only weak expert opinion that does not distinguish between any of the potential values. Only when there is bona fide expertise to influence the analysis does this Bayesian approach really come into its own.

Another extreme situation could be when the experts think they know the parameter value ahead of time in an absolute fashion. For the purposes of analysis, the appropriate beta distribution could be reflected as a mean of 0.05 but with essentially zero standard deviation. In such a scenario, it would make the expert opinion embedded in the analysis equivalent to a very large, or even infinite, number of data points. Although this kind of ultra-precision is probably not recommended, it does demonstrate that under certain circumstances the big data analysis can never hope to compete with exact expert knowledge.

The exact balance between the strength of expert opinion and the size of the data set will clearly depend on the details of the study, but it should be clear that this explicit incorporation of expert opinion into the analysis can be important. Notice also that the situation does not have to be as simple as the example that is presented here. With a more complicated model, the advantages of expert opinion can become even more valuable. This can be especially important when some observations are rare or difficult to obtain through random sampling. One such area is the analysis of reliability data, such as is discussed in Chapter 7.

Model Selection Impact

Another possible effect of using big data is that the number of variables in the set will increase as the sample size grows. In this case, the simple example that is given previously would have to be expanded to include many more columns of information for analysis.

For example, you might have 20 independent variables, $x1$ through $x20$, and one dependent variable y. If you do not have an expert opinion to guide the choice, then you may simply have to try all combinations of these variables to search for the best model. But, as has been argued previously, this can lead to an incredible computational load. Even if you limit the models to just five variables selected from the 20 candidates, it would still require checking more than 20,000 different potential models. If you would allow all possible models, then the amount of effort that is required could soon outrun the abilities of any computer. On the other hand, if the experts can already pare down the number of variables to a reasonable subset, then this will have enormous influence on the efficiency and efficacy of what the analysis can do. Even more complicated models can produce other challenges when you depend on the data alone to guide the analysis.

It is also worth mentioning that the same kind of effect, namely the incorporation of expert opinion into the analysis, can be essential for the separation of causal relationships from those that are merely correlational. Most users of statistical methods understand that numerical correlation cannot be assumed to be evidence of a true underlying physical causative relationship, but it is not as well known that methods have been developed to tease these two types of relationships apart. But, as currently developed, this causal analysis[27] requires the experts to outline the possible physical relationships that could occur in a system independently of the data at hand. Then the analysis combines the data and the presumed possible causal relationship to verify the results. Clearly, this approach cannot even begin if expert opinion is disallowed as a matter of principle, as suggested by the big data approach.

Causal Analysis

This close correspondence between expert knowledge and an effective sample size enables one to directly evaluate the apparent advantages of big data. After all, the assumption is that bigger data sets, more observations, and more variables are sufficient for producing good analyses. You have seen that this assumption can be undercut by the impact of missing values and other problems; however, in absence of these issues, you can see the merits more clearly.

As the Bayesian examples have shown, knowledge can be equated to data in a sensible fashion, so you can ask more detailed questions about how this might happen in the case of big data. What are the requirements to assure knowledge can be created from data to be equivalent to expertise? This is, in some ways, the reverse of the effective sample size relationship. Expertise is equivalent to data, but is it always true that data are equal to expertise? The immediate answer seems to be that it cannot be so in all cases. If you observe 100,000 copies of the same data point, then this is certainly not equivalent to the more robust knowledge gained from a more representative sampling. In this example, the data must be able to produce knowledge that is equivalent to the prior specification to be most useful. But this implies that you specify a beta distribution and a binomial likelihood, which is not directly obtainable from the data.

You could feasibly store the observed frequencies of the data, but this is not exactly the same as expressing the information as a beta distribution. In this case, the prior expressed as an unknown distribution would not be able to take advantage of the conjugate distribution properties that were the basis of the calculations provided in the numerical example. This, in turn, would mean the Bayesian procedure would have to be approximated by numerical methods. Since most software implementations of this approach require a named distribution to be specified, such as normal, binomial, etc., you would be faced with additional problems that could not be solved with the data alone. You are, once again, faced with the dilemma of having to provide extra information to guarantee that data-derived patterns are truly equivalent to knowledge.

Knowledge can usually be translated into equivalent data in a straight-forward fashion, but it could be more difficult to work this process in reverse to create knowledge from data.

7

Censored Data

The topic of censored data, briefly touched upon in earlier chapters, will be covered in more depth here. To illustrate the idea of censoring, we can consider a particular product, such as an incandescent lightbulb, which can fail to perform for a variety of reasons. The physical causes of the bulb's failure might include accidental breakage during handling, excessive environmental vibration, a surge in input power, or perhaps a filament that wore out from extended use. In each case, the occurrence of any one of these conditions could remove the bulb from service. The occurrence of any one reason for failure could also completely prevent the observation of failure for any of the other reasons when the failure is destructive, as is assumed here. That is, if the bulb is broken during the shipping process before it is even installed, then it cannot fail due to wearing out, vibration, or any of the other alternate causes. Whatever potential failure times might have been observed for one of the other causes, they will be censored because of the occurrence of the first type of failure. It is common to call these causes of failure the *failure modes*, and they are a mainstay of analysis in lifetime data and reliability applications.[28]

A numerical example can help illustrate this concept more clearly. Consider the case of just two possible failure modes that are competing with one another to see which will be the first cause that results in failure. Table 7.1 demonstrates the results that can occur from simulating the potential ages at death in years of 20 individuals who are assumed to be subjected to two particular mortality mechanisms. All these are simulated values that could be observed if censoring were not active. In any practical data set, including any that may be used in big data, only the values contained in the observed column would be available for analysis. As previously discussed, it is only through the use of these simulated values that you can appreciate the full ramification that can be caused by the improper analysis of censored data. In real data, the longer (potential) failure times would be missing because of the effect of censoring. It is only by using simulated values that you can see what data are missing. Notice the observed data values (column 4) are the lesser of the two potential values because it is the earliest failure that is observed. The fourth column in the data set represents the minimum of the other two failure times in each row. It would be impossible to see or collect the information for the failure time of censored cause in reality.*

A Big Data Approach

Consider this kind of data analysis under a naïve big data approach. The data, taken on their own merits, provide no indication that censoring is active. It is likely, therefore, that the algorithm would simply divide the data by failure mode type and then analyze each data set separately. The big data approach would run into the same difficulties in choosing a distribution, as illustrated previously, but for this example we will assume a Weibull distribution has been identified. The Weibull distribution is common for failure time, and it generally has two parameters of interest. The first, which is called the *shape*, reflects the type of physical mechanism that is involved in the failure, and its value determines the overall look of the distribution. The second parameter, which is called the *scale*, represents the 66.3 percentile point. It is often the scale parameter that is more interesting, since it reflects the middle of the distribution in a similar way as a mean or median. It is the scale parameter that is often used to help guide product development, set warranty limits, or write field manuals.

If the big data analysis uses the data separated by each unique failure mode to estimate the appropriate Weibull parameters, we could get the results that are given in Table 7.2. The resulting scale parameter estimates for disease and for accident are tagged separately as being naïve estimates, since they do not take into account censoring. Because these are simulated data, we also know something that is not normally available to the analyst, namely what the true values of the scale parameters are that were used

---

*This book will not go into detail about the methods that have been developed for handling censored data. Some of the assumptions that support the methodology are the independence of the failure mechanisms and the shared range of their operation. This area of statistical methodology is well-developed; *Practical Engineering, Process, and Reliability Statistics* by Mark Allen Durivage is a good source of information.

Table 7.1 Example of simulated censored data.

Individual number	Disease type	Accident type	Observed cause of death	Cause of death
1	10	89	10	Disease
2	26	62	26	Disease
3	4	7	4	Disease
4	28	40	28	Disease
5	27	51	27	Disease
6	39	78	39	Disease
7	45	8	8	Accident
8	24	2	2	Accident
9	13	12	12	Accident
10	26	13	13	Accident
11	34	55	34	Disease
12	43	1	1	Accident
13	63	9	9	Accident
14	45	56	45	Disease
15	26	17	17	Accident
16	12	1	1	Accident
17	27	10	10	Accident
18	31	50	31	Disease
19	8	33	8	Disease
20	15	66	15	Disease

in generating the random values. These true scale parameters are listed in Table 7.2. It is also possible to estimate the Weibull scale parameter using the 20 simulated values to mimic the impact the sampling error might do on its own, independently of the censoring effect. Table 7.2 contains these estimates as well, and they are called the *estimated values*. Finally, there are columns in the table that show the percent differences between the various values.

Table 7.2 Naïve estimates of the Weibull scale.

Disease				
True	Naïve	Estimated	PDTrueEst	PDTrueNaïve
30	27.29	31.64	–5.5%	7.4%
Accident				
True	Naïve	Estimated	PDTrueEst	PDTrueNaïve
40	8.75	39.09	2.3%	78.1%

The numbers in Table 7.2 indicate an alarming potential problem. First, the percent differences for the naïve approach (7.4% and 78.1%) are quite large, especially for the accident mode. Since the naïve errors are larger than the errors of the estimated values (–5.5% and 2.3%), this seems to indicate an additional error beyond what would be expected from sampling error alone. Normally, this naïve approach will result in a bias in the values as well. Next, the naïve estimates are always less than the true values, which again hint at the presence of bias. The actual amount of bias that can be created depends on the interplay of the failure modes, but it can be quite large for causes that are rare and that occur only later in life. The big data approach would likely produce values that are similar to the naïve ones given in this example.

Statisticians have developed a methodology to overcome the unintended bias that can develop when analyzing censored data. The basic idea of this correction is to combine all the data into one data set and then use the observed failure times for the mode of interest, such as the disease mode, as observed data and for all other failure modes (accident in the example) as censored information. Although most of the information about the censored data is hidden, it is known that whatever the failure time would have been observed (if it could be observed), it would have to be greater than the observed failure time. That is, in this example, when a person dies of disease, then the potential death time by accident would have to be greater than the observed value if it were to occur. This partial information is enough to correct for most of the potential bias if you employ the correct methods. Once the analysis is completed on one failure mode, then you reverse the roles of each mode and repeat the analysis to obtain the parameter estimates for the alternate modes (the accident mode). Table 7.3 repeats some of the older information and combines it with the properly corrected estimate of the scale parameter for each of the two failure modes.

Table 7.3   Naïve and corrected estimates of the Weibull parameters.

Disease						
True	Naïve	Estimated	Corrected	PDTrueEst	PDTrueNaïve	PDTrueCorr
30	27.29	31.64	28.94	–5.50%	7.4%	3.5%
Accident						
True	Naïve	Estimated	Corrected	PDTrueEst	PDTrueNaïve	PDTrueCorr
40	8.75	39.09	45.44	2.3%	78.1%	13.6%

In this example, the censored analysis does a better job of estimating the true scale parameters than the naïve approach does. The improvement is quite dramatic in the case of accidental deaths because it is here that the bias is most prominent. Again, the actual performance improvement offered by this approach will depend on the circumstances of the failure modes and how they interact—but in general, the bias can be reduced significantly by this approach compared to what might normally be suffered in a big data analysis.

Shortcomings of Big Data and Censoring

Since a big data approach cannot detect the impact of censoring from the data alone, it is unlikely to analyze the data correctly. It will likely proceed by dividing the original large data set into smaller subsets based on the different failure modes. The prototypical 100,000-point data set might be split into two approximately 50,000-point data sets in a situation with only two possible failure modes. This, by itself, is a problem for the big data rationale, but the problem can grow worse in more realistic situations. Most failures will have more than two physical failure mechanisms, perhaps more like 10 or so in total.

For example, the mortality data might have ages of death identified by accident type or disease type, which could quickly increase the number of modes to be analyzed. It is likely that the largest data sets will have more failure modes expressly because they will tend to have more variables, and this will simply exacerbate the problem. The strongest big data proponents aim for as much variety in their data sets as possible. If the data are divided evenly across the failure modes, then the working data sets might be on the order of 10,000 points, which, although large, is still likely to negate many of the benefits of big data. It is more likely that some of the rare failure modes will have much fewer observed values than the more common, faster-acting types, and so the smallest subsets of data used in the naïve approach could be much smaller than 10,000. For example, mortality from a rare disease type might have only a few instances even in a relatively large data set. And if that disease tends to manifest itself later in life, then it will be even more rarely included in the observed data. If the likelihood of seeing rare failure types is only 0.1%, for example, then the subset may be more like 100 observations that is used in the big data analysis. We can argue that larger data sets will likely capture rarer and rarer failure modes more often and thus raise the likelihood of having a few smaller subsets.

It is typical for failures to have different mechanisms that can extend over the potential lifespan of the device or individual. That is, in terms of the Weibull distribution, you should expect major differences between the scale parameters and perhaps in the shape parameters as well. The modes with the larger scale parameters will tend to occur at the end of the potential life rather than at the beginning, so they will likely have the least number of observations in the data set. Only the few rare cases that fail early from these longer-lived problems will appear in the observed data. Such situations are likely to lead to the largest biases.

The late failure modes have many more chances of being censored because the other failure modes are likely to occur earlier in the process.

Sometimes, it is these rare cases that can be of most importance, so any improper analysis can lead to costly mistakes. For example, if the rare disease is particularly contagious, then misjudging its true prevalence can lead to public health disasters. It is also likely that extremely rare modes will not be seen at all unless data sets are large or specialized methods are used in the sampling process.

Correcting the Bias Problem

With a large enough data set, even the rare failure modes should exhibit more uncensored observations in the data set—but this does not automatically correct the biasing problem, because the preponderance of observations that are obtained for these rare cases will be the early failures and will not, in general, contain any of the observations from the upper side of the distribution. If you do not consider this censoring effect, then clearly the estimates should still be biased to values that are much lower than what would be obtained if the full distribution were sampled. For example, a rare cause of death that occurs only at advanced ages may lead to a minimum of observed times substantially lower than typical values, which can lead the analyst to attribute more importance to this cause than might be warranted. Eventually, it can be an insidious problem making it nearly impossible to gather uncensored data, which means the bias may go undetected for a long time.

Consider also the impact of collecting data over the long time periods that are often necessary to create the massive data repositories that are assumed for big data. Very few products will remain unchanged long-term. For example, new versions of the product may be introduced or subtle engineering changes could be made along the way. Even modifications of administrative processes such as warranties or replacement policies can impact the observed times that individual items are removed from service.

If the observations are obtained from products in the field, then the introduction times may vary, as well as the severity of usage. Therefore, it is likely that the failure mode behaviors will change with time as well in big data sets. The user of big data is, once again, faced with the dilemma of trying to isolate subsets of the data that are consistent within themselves, and this can lead to formidable challenges. The choice seems to be between reducing the data set size, accepting whatever errors occur due to instability, or applying (by default) a more complicated analysis.

There are more flexible types of censored analysis, called *life regression*, that can make the scale parameter a function of background variables that could be used. But now, the naïve big data approach has to select a model using all the available variables (and functional forms), which is nearly impossible in its own right based on the data alone. Without the incorporation of expert knowledge (not contained in the data at hand), this is nearly impossible to achieve. Even the extensive use of validation sets is unlikely to fix this problem since the same kind of censoring is likely to dominate in the held-over subsets as well.

In the mortality data example presented in this chapter, it is assumed that the big data analysis would use a typical lifetime distribution such as the Weibull for the analysis; but, from a strict viewpoint, this would depend on expert opinion. If you are not privy to this guidance, then the same issues about choosing a distribution that were investigated earlier come into play. The big data analysis procedure would somehow have to select the distribution based on the data alone. Thus, the approach could result in choosing completely different distributions for each different failure mode, which can eliminate many of the advantages of using a fixed and known distribution and may make the bias correction procedure impossible to apply. It is also possible to have different types of censoring that are simultaneously active in the data set, such as interval censoring, which may have to be handled in a different way than what has been discussed. These decisions and choices will not be easy for the big data analysis to negotiate without having any access to human contextual knowledge.

In practical situations, it is usually possible to select likely distribution and even likely values for Weibull-shape parameters based on the physical nature of the failure mode. For example, random failure is usually best modeled as shape equal to one. In a similar way, it is possible to provide expert opinion as to the possible shape parameter values that can then be used to improve the analysis. For example, you can use Bayesian methods similar to those discussed in Chapter 6 to do analysis without any observed failures (or a small number of them). These options would seem to be unavailable to any big data analysis that refuses to incorporate expert opinion.

In summary, censoring presents an extreme case of the challenges of missing values for big data analysis approaches. Because the correction of the data for censoring can involve assumptions about the distributions behind the system, it is hard to see how a naïve big data approach can make this choice based only on a data search. Recognizing the need for treating the data in a different fashion must come from knowing the physical nature of the data in the study, and this, currently at least, assumes the existence of a human analyst.

8

Other Potential Problems

Up to now, we have detailed some of the major challenges that can be encountered when trying to use naïve big data analysis to analyze data. To round out the potential problems, we will present a brief survey of other issues that may arise in this context. The fundamental problem that underlies these challenges is similar to that faced before, namely, the reluctance of big data to allow the introduction of context-sensitive information into the analysis. Although we have chosen to treat these additional challenges in much less detail than we have done with the previous ones, it should not be considered an indicator of their potential seriousness. The potential problems in this chapter can occur frequently in modern data sets and can have a serious impact just as any of the others discussed up to this point.

The Treatment of Outliers

It can be quite common in data sets of any size to have some observations that look so unusual they might be considered outliers. Outliers are observations that do not belong to the distribution that corresponds to the process or system that is of interest.[29] As a case in point, you may be interested in estimating the natural capability of the manufacturing process. In most cases, this capability should reference the normal, well-functioning performance of the system and not focus on various process upsets that may occur. However, in a specific data collection you may accidentally include some of the information from process upset conditions. It is possible for just a few of these abnormal data points to completely change the results, and they might be considered as outliers for this case.

In many ways, the definition of an outlier is similar to one given for a weed: a good plant in the wrong place. For example, if you are expecting to find only the numbers 0 to 10 in a set of data, then the appearance of a value of 15 might indicate a potential outlier. The trouble dealing with outliers is how to tell reliably whether the value is unusual or if it is simply a very rare occurrence under what otherwise should be considered as typical behavior. Regardless of what you do with the outlier in the final analysis, it is almost always beneficial to do a thorough investigation of the outlier to better understand its occurrence in the data.

Investigating the causes for the unusual data can often be rewarding by itself. But, for our purposes, the importance of an outlier lies in the potential negative impact for the big data treatment. Even the seemingly simple example just given of the errant number 15 can be difficult for the big data approach. Since the big data approach prefers not to make assumptions about the data, there are no immediate criteria on which you can decide that a value of 15 is unusual. The algorithm is forced to develop criteria for outlier determination based only on the data at hand, and this can offer some difficulties. Typically, it will require some strong user input to validate one's decision about outliers. Consider the example in Table 8.1, which illustrates the problem.

Table 8.1 Outlier example.

1	12	17
18	13	6
9.1	28	11
–1	9	12
34	9	18

Consider the challenge of determining which, if any, of these 15 values should be treated as an outlier. Numerically, the value of 34 seems to be quite far from the rest of the data, but so does the number 28 to a lesser degree. And what do you make of the negative number that occurs? Why does only one value have a decimal point? Any of these discrepancies could signal that something unusual is happening in the case of these particular values, but how can you tell this simply from the data themselves? It seems clear that something about the physical setup must be provided to decide some of these issues. For example, you may know that negative numbers are simply impossible in this system or that a decimal point is the result of a data integration problem. Such knowledge would give you more confidence that the negative number and the decimal number are unusual enough to be considered outliers. Even this kind of context-specific knowledge does not help much with determining the status of the numbers 34 and 28 so easily. Although it is possible that the physical constraints of the situation could also make these numbers infeasible, the explanation of their appearance is probably due to something more subtle happening. For example, they could signal true process upsets or mistakes, but they also could represent a very rare but acceptable set of running conditions.

Since potential outliers are a common problem in realistic data sets, numerous statistical approaches have been developed to try to identify outliers.[30] Being statistical in nature, these tests are based on estimating probabilities that candidate data points are different from the assumed distribution. One typical approach is to identify a potential outlier, such as the value 34, and then calculate the parameters of the distribution based on the remaining 12 numbers (assuming the negative number and the decimal number have been removed already from the set).

In most cases, the distribution must be preassigned to complete the test calculation, and, as we have seen, this is an additional challenge for the big data approach. But assuming that such a distribution has been chosen, say as a normal distribution, then you can use a rule based on the normal distribution to determine how unusual the value of 34 appears. If the value of 34 is far from the observed mean of the reduced distribution, then it is a good candidate to be considered an outlier. This judgment is not exact, however, and you must decide the level of probability to use to justify excising this value from the data set. Notice that this approach still includes the other candidate outlier 28 in the data set when the baseline is computed for testing the value of 34. If the value of 28 is also an outlier, then clearly its inclusion in the baseline will affect your ability to judge the legitimacy of the value 34.

There are methods in which groups of outliers can be considered simultaneously, but you still need to identify the candidates upfront. It is hard to see exactly how the big data analysis approach would work to identify the potential outliers without some assumptions about the data. In most cases, the determination of potential outliers is a judgment call. Notice also that this approach must work on both ends of the scale, and things become even more complicated if you suspect that the value of 1 that appears in the example data set might be an outlier as well.

You might ask about the consequences of leaving outliers in the analysis. Although there are techniques to do robust analyses without removing the outliers, it is more likely that any big data approach would simply leave these abnormal values in the data hoping the preponderance of typical data would swamp their effects. To see that this might not be the case, we can simply look at the set of 15 values that are given in the example data set. If we remove the negative value and reread 9.1 as 9, then the calculated average of the remaining 14 values is 14.07. Assuming the two bigger outlier candidates are removed, the recalculated average on the smaller set of data will have the new value of 11.35. This is a difference of nearly 3 out of a range of 17, which likely is not inconsequential.

If the candidate outlier values are even more extreme, this could lead to even bigger deviations. It is not hard to see that even one outlier, when it is extreme enough, can change the entire analysis drastically. For example, consider the impact with an unusual value of 34,000 instead of 34. The impact of leaving outliers in the data set can be extreme under the right conditions.

It is still possible, however, that the sheer number of data points that are assumed in the big data approach could work in its favor, but this is likely not the case. Outliers are assumed to be samples taken from an aberrant distribution (or distributions) that happen to appear in the data set. Thus, the occurrence of outliers is likely to be associated with actual processes that are occurring simultaneously alongside the system of interest during the collection of the data. The number of outliers, therefore, depends on how often these alternate processes occur. Clearly, the answer will depend on the details of the situation, but it is probably not unreasonable to assume that the probability of an outlier occurs at a consistent rate across the entire data collection. This would certainly be the case if the errors were due to misreads on embedded sensors or typographical mistakes.

It could also be the case if the outliers were due to some periodic interruptions like new batches of raw materials or incorrect operator behavior. A similar thing would be true if the outliers were generated by process interruptions or accidents. If the assumption of a consistent frequency of outlier occurrence proves to be correct, then it would probably not be unexpected to see the same proportion of outliers in any data set, no matter its size. If you consider the example data set in which there are four likely outliers out of the total of 15 data points, then this could mean that outliers occur at a rate of 4 divided by 15, or just under 25%. If you were to extrapolate this rate to the prototypical 100,000-value data set, then you could have nearly 25,000 potential outliers. Determining the status of so many candidates could easily become a numerical nightmare for any big data analysis. This high rate of outliers is probably unrealistically large, but even a rate of 1% could be a challenge. For the case of 100,000 observations, this lower rate could still mean that there were nearly 1,000 potential outliers to be investigated.

How is the big data algorithm going to decide how to proceed with the task of outlier identification? Somehow, it must be able to parse through many different subsets depending on how many outliers are under simultaneous test. You would have to investigate one-point cases (two of them), two-point scenarios (three of them), three-point cases (four of them), and so on up to and including 1,000-point scenarios (around 1,001 of them), even in a case in which all outliers are thought to be taken from the extremes of the observed data. And there is no way to know that 1,000 is the maximum value in this search because more (or fewer) outliers could be possible in a circumstance, and that alone could lead to a lot of extra work that would be necessary before the true big data analysis process could begin.

Keep in mind that, throughout this process, each answer is likely to be stated in probabilistic terms, and so you still need an expert opinion to determine what is a suitable cutoff for these tests. And without some expert guidance, even these approaches might miss the more context-sensitive errors that are presented in the existence of negative numbers or decimals, as illustrated in the example.

As the data-set size grows, it is likely to suffer more damage from outliers rather than less. The collection of extremely large data sets typically requires new modes of data capture, and each new mode could introduce another mechanism for creating outliers. For example, if data collection speed were suddenly increased to capture more data, then data dropouts might become more prevalent. Or, if collection times were extended to include startup conditions or process upsets, then this might also introduce new subprocesses into the mix, each with its own unique set of issues.

In the case that the large data set is constructed through the merger of smaller ones, then it is likely that new conditions will be introduced in the final data set. Since it is assumed that big data repositories have more variables, this also increases the chance of unusual behavior in some of the data table columns. Rarer events will more likely be captured for both the desired distribution as well as the outlier distributions. If the stability of the data is in question, then it will also be more difficult to pick adequate baseline distributions on which to base the outlier tests. Uncertainty about the number of outliers and their distributions can turn the big data analysis approach to detecting outliers into a daunting task.

Missing Data Issues

An interesting way to look at the potential effect of outliers on the big data analysis is to view them as the reverse of the missing data issue. In the case of missing data, we lose information in ways that could affect the analysis adversely, and big data simply does not take account of this. In the case of outliers, it is the reverse situation, where we include excess observations that could adversely affect the analysis. A common feature of the two situations is that the big data approach has no easy way to deal with either issue. The only workable approach seems to be to include a set of additional algorithms that are used to detect and eliminate the outliers before the proper analysis is performed, but this approach clearly requires the inclusion of expert opinion to make it workable. Without this set of guiding principles that is sourced separately from the data at hand, it is easy to see that big data results will be very sensitive to the particular characteristics of each data set that is presented. This also makes it unlikely that the results will fit well on validation data sets or project reliably into future conditions.

It is also likely that the outlier behavior could vary among the different variables that are sampled to construct the big data set. If you have a couple hundred variables in the 100,000-point data set, then you would have to apply the search procedure again and again for each variable. The variable with the most frequent occurrence of outliers would likely force the analyst to delete data (full rows in the data set) to accommodate these worst cases, and this could eventually reduce the data-set size dramatically. One variable at a 10% outlier generation rate could reduce the size of the original from 100,000 to 90,000 as a result. And, if you consider that all the outliers could be randomly scattered throughout the data, you could easily lose even more data.

This is similar to what was discussed earlier with respect to missing values, in which even a small rate of occurrence for each variable could lead to big losses over the full set. If each variable has a 10% chance of seeing an outlier independently wrong the other columns, then a data set with many variables (say a hundred or more) could accidentally lose most of its rows in this way. The chance that no variable will experience an outlier in this situation would be near $0.90^{50} \sim 0.005$, which means only 0.5% of the original 100,000 rows or about 500 might be retained. This would certainly be restrictive for the big data analysis and might even be prohibitive. And if the number of variables climbs higher to 100, for example, the problem becomes so bad that no data might be retained at all; that is, $0.90^{100} * 100,000 \sim$ three retained rows. Having 100 variables is certainly not out of the question for some big data analysis scenarios, so the problem might turn out to be dramatic.

Decision Error

Another perhaps more subtle issue that can arise when dealing with large data sets is the assessment of decision error. If the purpose of the analysis is to predict behavior on an as-yet-unknown set of data, then there will always be some chance of making an error when the fitted model is used to predict these new cases. When this error is assumed to be stochastic in nature, we have argued that one way or another, you must have some kind of baseline statistical distribution to frame the analysis. Considered in this way, you must think about the data at hand, regardless of size, as merely representative of the potentially infinite sets of data that could be collected. These kinds of errors are labeled as decision errors in this text because they represent mistakes that could be made when decisions are predicated on the erroneous analysis.

The general approach to evaluating decision errors is to compare any given result with what is expected under the assumption of a particular distribution to determine the probabilities that decision errors may occur. This leads to the standard Type 1 and Type 2 errors that most people are familiar with from an introductory course in statistical methods. The most important feature of this approach to evaluating decision errors, for our purposes, is the fact that they are typically functions of the number of samples, that is, the sample size. Such dependence can be good or bad. It is this dependence of errors on the sample size that can give big data analysis the ability to determine differences with amazingly enhanced precision, but the same dependence can lead to some unexpected issues.

As an example of the sample size dependence of these approaches, we need only consider the well-known relationship between the standard deviation of an average and the standard deviation of individual results. The standard deviation of the average of a set of independent samples is expected to be smaller than the individual standard deviation in the ratio of the inverse of the square root of sample size. Numerically, this would mean the standard deviation of the average of four samples is expected to be equal to the individual standard deviation divided by the square root of four when evaluated over the infinite samples that are potentially obtainable. Thus, you can detect differences that are one half the original size of what can be studied with individual values simply by switching to averages of four samples. This is a very powerful feature upon which most statistical methods are built, and the same is true for most methods of statistical learning.

The potential trouble for big data comes into play because this relationship between precision and sample size can continue indefinitely. A sample size of 16 would be expected to bring the standard deviation down to one quarter of its original size, and a sample size of 100 would be expected to bring it down to one tenth of its original size. Using the prototypical 100,000 data points, to which we have been referring as representative of the big data approach, this would mean that detectable differences would be as small as $1/\sqrt{(100,000)} \sim 1/316 \sim 0.003$ of those available for individual values. Even larger data sets would mean greater sample sizes, which could lead, invariably, to even greater reductions. Although such enhanced precision might initially seem to be invariably positive, it can actually lead to some complications when the data analyst tries to use the results.

The ultra-sensitivity of large data sets can sometimes lead to disconnects when comparing the results analyses gained from the big data approach to expectations based on more standard analysis. For example, the construction of control charts and capability indices usually requires the calculation of a test of normality to be applied to the data. The results of applying this test on a typical set of 100 to 120 values that is often recommended for capability studies can be quite different from that achieved by applying it to 100,000 values. With the larger data set, the test can detect very small departures from expectation, which can be much finer than those that are testable using the smaller samples size of 120. One need only compare the reduction power of 1/316 to 1/10 to see that the large data set can detect differences that are 316/10 = 31.6 times finer. This ability to detect smaller significant departures will often lead us to reject the adequacy of the normal distribution even when the fit is visibly close. Because of the sensitivity of the big data results, small discrepancies due to rounding rules can often determine the results of the distribution tests.

Other common problems that can arise could be caused by gaps in the data or the truncation of distribution tails. Since it is also difficult to collect so many data points without encountering some instability, you may see subtle bimodal patterns more readily. It can be difficult for the user of such counter-intuitive results to know how to proceed. One possibility is that the user can accept the large sample size result directly and act on the results just as they are presented. This most likely would lead the user to proceed as if the data are non-normal. The next steps would depend on how the company treats capability for non-normal data, but in most cases, this means you must use less-desirable indicators such as performance rather than capability, or you may need to apply non-normal indices in the calculation. The use of non-normal indices is likely to bring additional problems because the sensitivity provided by 100,000 data values will probably result in the rejection of any of the standard distributions (named) that are available in the software. It is possible to substitute less powerful nonparametric methods at this point, but this is not without problems either.

Another option when faced with the rejection of normality because of the enhanced sensitivity of big data is to purposely reduce the sample size that is used in the distribution test to something that matches more closely to the lower expected sample size of 100 to 120. However, this clearly goes against the grain of what big data analysis is all about. It also can suffer from the problem that different subsamples may yield different results for the test, so there could be an issue deciding on a sampling plan in the first place. Again, any additional problems that might arise from instability can make this subset selection even more problematic.

A third approach is to demand a smaller level of Type 1 errors to overcome the extra precision that is obtainable from the larger data set, but these kinds of corrections would seem to demand that some level of expert knowledge is added into the process. Besides, this kind of adjustment is certainly not standardized in the literature for this kind of problem. The company practitioner might find it necessary to introduce new methodology for a common application before proceeding to get a final answer, not to mention any issues such idiosyncratic methods might raise for external auditors.

Some defenders of the big data approach may argue that these decision errors only exist when standard statistical methods are applied, but it is hard to justify this approach. It is certainly true that you do not have to assign a statistical distribution to the possible samples, but without some systematic approach, it will be difficult to gauge performance. The use of a verification set is helpful, but since it will always be finite in size, you are left with the same problem of how to deal with the potentially infinite sets of data points that are not observed. If you can still make errors in applying fitted models to these as-yet-unknown samples, then you can still make the two types of errors. It might be possible to adapt the definitions of Type 1 and Type 2 errors without referring to probabilities, but overall content of the approach would seem nearly universal. That is, if you can make errors, then they will be of the two types that are described by these labels.

At heart, there is always a chance of false positives or false negatives when the data are not exhaustive. If the connection that exists between the sampled observations and the infinite number of possible observations is treated stochastically, then something like probabilities are likely to be involved. On the other hand, it is feasible to create tests that are not dependent on sample size for their precision, but this would seem to negate the potential advantages of big data if they were to be used in the analysis. Indeed, it would seem to prohibit almost all forms of useful analysis. If more data are not seen as better, you should question the validity of the approach no matter what the mathematical details might be. Besides, it is not the inherent ability of large data sets to offer better precision in decision-making that is the fundamental issue but rather the ability to make good decisions based on this increased precision in the results. One can argue that the two characteristics of bias and precision will be crucial measures of performance no matter what the approach is, and it is these two objectives that are at the heart of the comparison between informed analysis and the naïve big data approach.

Model Complexity

Another issue comes into play because of the assumption that big data repositories will likely see an expansion of the number of variables that are available for analysis in addition to an increased number of observations. We have already seen the potential negative impacts of this increase in the number of variables in some of the other chapters. Again, it is the situation that while more information is intuitively richer, it is necessary to manage this extra potential in a smart manner. The lesson of much of the book is a justification that subject-area information is useful and often critical for this purpose. We will try to expand the discussion of this issue of the challenge offered by an abundance of variables in the section.

As a simple example of the impact of more variables on decisions, we can consider a simple data set with only four variables a, b, c, and d. If you are trying to find an adequate model for a particular response variable, then there are 14 different (linear) models (ignoring the intercept only model and the null model) that can be contemplated. These models can be listed as the following set of combinations:

a, b, c, d, $a+b$, $a+c$, $a+d$, $b+c$, $b+d$, $c+d$, $a+b+c$, $a+b+d$, $c+b+d$, and $a+b+c+d$.

The shorthand used here equates $c+d$ to the model coef1*c + coeff2*d and so on. Although linear models are used here to make the point, the same worries extend to nonlinear and complicated (activation functions) as well. Most modern software can easily be used to fit each of these potential models to determine which individual model seems to be the best.

If these data are still assumed to be a representative sample from a potentially infinite set of possible data, there is always some kind of possible error in choosing the correct model. Often in this situation, the significance level is used to determine which model is best fitted by the data. Each comparison or decision on a model structure has an associated chance of making this kind of error. Often the cutoff value of a Type 1 error rate at 0.05 is used to distinguish between acceptable models and those that are not as acceptable. The trouble begins when you use the data to make multiple decisions in this way because each individual decision has this same chance of error. So, the chance of making an error, when accumulated over the multiple decisions that are made on the data set, can be larger than this assigned value for a single comparison. To distinguish between the two types of errors, the individual decision errors are often called *comparison-wise errors*, and the overall error is designated as the *experiment-wise error*.[31] When there are many decisions made in a study, it is likely that this experiment-wise error rate can grow quite large.

The general calculation of the experiment-level error can be done from knowledge of the comparison-level error and the number of comparisons that are performed by using the formula experiment-wise error rate = $1 - (1-\text{comparison-wise error rate})^{\text{number of comparisons}}$. If we apply this formula to the example situation that was discussed in the previous paragraph, then the experiment-wise error rate will be $1 - (1-0.05)^{14} = 1 - (0.95)^{14} = 0.51$. So, instead of maintaining an error rate of 1 out of 20, the real error rate is 1 out of 2. This same kind of multiplication of errors should impact any methods of making these kinds of decisions that operate under the assumption that we are trying to predict an infinite number of possibilities from a sample. Of course, non-probabilistic approaches may have different ways of calculating the error rates, but the impact should be similar.

One way to combat the problem is to strengthen the initial error-rate requirement from 0.05 downward to 0.01. This change would make the overall (experiment-wise) error rate around 13%, which might make the situation more acceptable. Of course, you can use the equation to solve for the appropriate comparison-wise error rate, which will achieve whatever target experiment-wise error rate you have in mind. It should be noted that an expert opinion is likely involved in the selection of the level of error that is acceptable, both on the comparison level and the experimental level.

It is likely in the case of big data analysis that the number of variables will be larger than the simple set of four that is used in the illustration. One of the stronger selling points for these approaches is that big data repositories are striving to include as many variables as possible. It is hard to say exactly how many new variables to expect, since each situation will be idiosyncratic, but it is probably not unreasonable to expect that you might add one new variable for every 100 new data points. If this were the case, then our prototypical 100,000-point data set could have 1,000 variables. It now becomes practically impossible to test all the possible models that could be created from combinations of these 1,000 variables. Even if you restricted the models to be of one, two, or three variables, then the total number of models is on the order of 166,667,500. If we use 100,000 in the formula for the calculation of total error, then we would have to reduce the error rate for any comparison from 5% down to something like 0.0000000005 to hold the line on potential errors to something reasonable.

This would seem to be a real dilemma for big data analysis since decisions about model complexity, such as the number of variables that should be involved, smacks of incorporating expert opinion rather than depending entirely on the data set at hand. Of course, these calculations only cover linear combination of the variables. Naïve big data analysis should have no preference for the model type and, seemingly, must search through all polynomial models and nonlinear models using the same variables.

Consideration of more complicated models only complicates the problem. For the example of four variables, we saw how there were 14 linear combinations of the variables to consider. In making this statement, we are using linear to be in the mathematical sense of being of linear in the variables. Statistical models, being linear in the parameters, can also include cross-products, powers, and other terms and still be considered linear. But if we allow nonlinear models, then the number of possible models quickly escalates to the point of being theoretically infinite. You could have models only using a variable in any power from 1 to infinite, for example, or as logs to any conceivable base. Of course, you would likely have to restrict this choice of possible models in some way; there are clearly a lot of new options. A simple search strategy such as the one described previously for the linear example would be impossible without some overall, simplifying plan of attack. And as we have seen over and over in our discussions, this would require expert input that is not found within the data on their own merits.

Accumulation of Knowledge

Big data analysis would also seem to have a problem with the accumulation of knowledge. Since each analysis is supposed to depend only on the data presented to it, there is no easy mechanism to incorporate what has been learned in older studies. For example, if an analysis has been performed on a data set with the original 100,000 values, then all results should likely be discarded when even an additional single observation is added to the data set. Although you might want to argue in favor of waiting until there is more than one update, this does not fit the contentions of big data. It is feasible that this single additional point could change the overall results drastically.

Establishing some kind of refresh rule in which the analysis is redone after any other threshold, say every 10 or 100 new observations, would be another instance of expert opinion. The same consideration would be true if you edited the original data or corrected them in some fashion. In the extreme case, each big data analysis must essentially recreate all knowledge each time it performs a new analysis. Since it is possible that each modified set of data could lead to different conclusions, the strictly data-centric approach would seem to have no choice but to redo the analysis often. To do otherwise seems to require that some extra information be added that is not inherent in the data.

Currently, knowledge is thought to be gained by iterating over a two-step process in which hypotheses are tested against data and updated as necessary. In applying this approach, the only thing retained from the first analysis is the fitted model form itself, perhaps with some summary measure of how well it fitted to the data. It is only in rare cases that the summarization would take more than a paragraph or two of text to capture. Compare this to the big data acquired information. Most likely, the safest procedure would be to store the model's details used, usually a complicated one, in addition to the full data set that was used in the analysis. Storing the details can be necessary because the models can be so intricately attached to the particular data that are used in the fitting process.

For example, the use of a deep learning neural network might require one to store all the multitude of nodes within their intricate network along with the estimated weights. Since the weights will, in general, change with any new input data, then it would seem that you would need to store the actual data values that were used to select these particular weights as well, which would have to be repeated for every iteration of the model. This could make the smooth growth of knowledge into something much more complicated and discontinuous. The need to capture explicit details of both the model-fitting process and the data is already a feature of many efforts. Often, the only real way to ensure that your work can be validated (or duplicated) is to provide direct access to the program and the data set. As a result, it can cause problems if a third party is performing the validation. In addition to possible security problems that might be involved, software licensing and training may be necessary if a third party is used. Issues with time and resources could also arise.

Philosophically, this new approach of data-sensitive results could go against the grain of the scientific method. Although the details of this method can vary to some degree from source to source, the general gist of the scientific approach is that there are several methodical steps that can be taken in an iterative fashion to gain understanding of the physical world. The method usually consists of four steps:

1. Collecting and collating previous information that is useful for the problem at hand

2. Using this information to create a hypothesis or model that can be applied to explain the data

3. Subjecting this hypothesis to test against new data through active experimentation

4. Combining this new information with historical results and restart the process

This is similar to, but expands upon, the discussion in the previous paragraphs. The two interlocking pieces of the puzzle appear prominently in this approach, namely, the use of previous information and its combination with new data. The strict application of the big data approach would seemingly lead to a different model of learning in comparison to this description. Since there is no explicit allowance for previous information to affect the analysis, one must rely entirely on the information contained in the current data set. Essentially, the hope seems to be that, if you are given enough data, then you can recreate the information each time the analysis is performed. It is even difficult to imagine what such a process would look like. Sometime, at point 1, the big data analyst would collect a specified data set of size $n1$ and fit model $m1$. Whenever sufficient new data have arrived (possibly at each new data point), a new analysis would be conducted at time $t2$ on data set 2 of size $n1+n2$. A new model $m2$ is fitted. If this new model is for the same purposes as the original, then it should be supposed that $m2$ would completely replace $m1$. But if the analysis were for a different purpose, then it is an open question whether $m1$ should be replaced by a new $m1$-improved.

As this process continues through subsequent analyses, you can envision an expanding tree of models, each with an associated data set of potentially ever-increasing size. Each time a new purpose is chosen or old model is updated, it would likely grow a bigger data set (accumulate the past ones). If the analyst chose not to update the old analyses, then it would probably be necessary to retain the old data set even though there is an updated version. That is the only way to reproduce the original results exactly. Thus, it is possible, in this scenario, that you would have to store multiple data sets as the analysis proceeded even though many of these would have only slight differences between them.

Clearly, it could become a logistical nightmare to store all these various versions and keep their uses straight. It is much more likely that the analyst would apply some simplifying logic to the process, perhaps by updating all models at each stage, but it needs to be stressed that this is another application of information from beyond the data at hand. Even if it were practically possible to continually build up data sets to the extent that they could capture all the current knowledge, there are even more challenges for this big data approach.

The previous example assumed there was a starting point at which the first model was constructed, but this is probably unrealistic. Even in the case of a brand-new start-up process of a company that is creating its first set of data, there is likely a plethora of information that is pertinent but that exists before the first data point is collected. There may be trial runs of the equipment or lab data from prototype development that are useful. All the training and experience of the people involved in the design of equipment and the initial installation is also potentially valuable. This prior expertise also should include any information in textbooks or lecture notes that has informed the development of the process to this point.

Practically, this kind of information is used throughout the process to frame issues and establish standards, but big data's over-reliance on only the data at hand puts it at a disadvantage. The use of the Bayesian methods that are described in Chapter 6 could explicitly address this problem, but the need to depend exclusively on data makes this methodology unavailable. Instead, it would seem that big data would require one to supply data that could be used to recreate all this knowledge. As was shown in Chapter 6, it is possible to transform knowledge into equivalent data to some degree. Whereas it was mostly the effective sample that was useful to convert, now you would have to create specific data that capture the knowledge and its degree of certainty. You can imagine the difficulty of recreating adequate data to capture a physical law, such as Newton's third law. Since this law is so well established as to be nearly certain, it would also have to contain a large number of data points to capture this level of confidence. In many cases, this constructed data would be much larger than the observed data no matter how extensive they might be. This problem is duplicated over all such known physical relationships that might be used. Indeed, the amount of data that might be necessary to truly support such knowledge might be infinite.

The critical difference in the approaches seems to be in the kinds of models that can be used to store knowledge. For most scientific work, the models are continuous in that they depend on real numbers for their definition. There is no way to reproduce perfectly the information of a continuum of points with any finite (however large) data set. Even if the values underlying real performance were just a countably infinite set, then this would still be an unreachable goal for the big data analysis to achieve. The only hope for ultimate big data success seems to rest on the possibility that most of the useful information about the operations of the world can be modeled with finite structures.

The final resolution of this issue would seem to depend on the nature of the physical world itself. Indeed, some philosophers consider it to be impossible to discover a new understanding relying only on data without a theoretical component. The basic argument is that the information gained from data cannot be greater than the information contained in the data, if that is all that can be used. Without models, one can be reduced to the proverbial situation of rearranging the deck chairs on the Titanic. Regardless of whether this general philosophical argument is true, it does seem that the chances of big data being able to duplicate the achievements of science to this point in history are rather low. And with each new fact that is generated, through any form of analysis, it is likely to make that task more difficult. Given the rate of advancement of knowledge, this seems to be a losing battle for the big data approach.

Although the points that are made in the previous discussion are probably valid, it is not our belief that this is a realistic view of what will actually happen. Indeed, for most applications of statistical learning on big data, data sets, there is a liberal use of expertise to set the problem and adapt the analysis to the purpose. This is not necessarily a bad thing. Rather, this direct interplay between information and data seems to be exactly the best route in which to proceed. The viewpoint that is expressed in this book is that the incorporation of additional information into an analysis is often necessary and usually desirable. The secret seems to be to understand how best to incorporate this additional understanding into the analysis no matter the size of the data set. It is the incorporation of growing knowledge, in addition to better methods of analysis, that is likely to be the key for future progress.

Some General Observations

One helpful way to imagine the process is to reconsider the idea of combining knowledge and new data from Chapter 6. In that case, it was expert knowledge that was considered, but similar effects occur with the incorporation of anything into the analysis that is not directly contained in the data at hand. It was argued that the best answer in some sense was a weighted average of the two sources of pertinent information. When knowledge was stronger than data, then the weighting was heavier on expertise, and vice versa in the reverse situation.

Given the relative sparsity of current big data compared to our accumulated knowledge, it would seem that we should continue to give more weight to the expertise in many cases. Certainly, it could be argued that it would often be foolish or at least inefficient to do otherwise. But in circumstances in which we truly are entering novel conditions, then perhaps data should be given preference, especially as data sets become larger. It is also feasible that one really does wish to avoid previous knowledge to gain a fresh perspective on a problem, but even in the limited way this is possible today, it does not seem to be a common problem of our target quality practitioner. To truly construct new results that are not dependent on assumptions and hidden expertise is a difficult task, like constructing a truly noninformative prior distribution.

Conclusion

There are a wide variety of challenges to the practical implementation of the big data approach in its attempts to eliminate the need for expert input. The very construction of an analytic data set is beset with enough challenges to almost ensure that our data sets will be compromised. We have seen the potentially devastating impact of ignoring missing data in our analyses and the likely biases that can result without correction. We compared the differences between actively manipulating a process as in a statistically designed experiment versus the passive data collection that is the mainstay of big data. We also examined the issues posed by poor randomization of data and the existence of censored data. All these issues can result in spurious conclusions and can create real harm. The chapter on Bayesian methods demonstrated a possible link between knowledge and data that can be used both to improve analyses and to characterize problems in the procedure. Finally, we tried to examine the philosophical difficulties that could be encountered by divorcing expertise and data.

Given the limitations of big data analytics, the average practitioner should be wary of accepting the most extravagant claims of big data at face value.

It is probably fair to say that, in most current applications, there is quite a bit of assumed knowledge that goes into constructing the models or fine-tuning them, with the actual amount depending on each example. In the case of the typical quality analyst, it is unlikely that the big data approach by itself can lead to anything nearly as successful as what an analyst is probably applying in his or her daily work today. More data are clearly desirable, but it is likely that they can only be used successfully when incorporating even more expert knowledge into the analysis. It is this matched procession of increased data plus increased knowledge that is the favored horse in this race.

Hopefully, the methodologies that are introduced in this book prove helpful to you in overcoming many of the common challenges faced when analyzing data of any kind—but especially if you are tempted to rely on the data alone. Perhaps the basic finding here is that big data is best considered as an enhancement for human experts rather than as a competition.

Predicting the future correctly is notoriously difficult, but there are some general trends within sight today that can be used to construct a reliable pathway for future work in this arena. First, it is clear that computer analysis will become more and more powerful with each passing year, and the rate of improvement is probably accelerating. Second, the analysis methodologies such as those described in this book, as well as other forms of statistical learning, will also continue to improve at a furious pace.

For the most part, the software side of the issue can be counted on to develop at an even faster rate than the hardware side. In mathematics, concepts are often developed before they can be performed practically. If we look at only these two trends, then we might conclude that big data is the ultimate objective; but this is probably an incorrect conclusion, because there is also a trend in the creation of knowledge that occurs simultaneously with these other two patterns. It is a good bet to assume that our creation of knowledge will either match or exceed the growth in these other areas, which seems to be the case since it is inherently cumulative in nature and usually takes the form of a continuous model. In some sense, each new hard-earned fact adds the equivalent of an infinite amount of data because of the models we use to summarize our knowledge. So, while we might argue that the fundamental rate of creating new knowledge is slower, we never lose it once we have gained it.

Therefore, the wisest course of action for the conscientious analyst is to do everything necessary to foster this growth of knowledge so as to always be ready to correct a data-myopic analysis if it has the chance of going astray. Since the development of the mathematical methods and computer implementations will continue unabated regardless of what the typical quality practitioner does, it is essential that development of knowledge be managed locally. Of course, this is not likely to be a simple trivial task; it is likely to be a critical one. Luckily, those individuals who are currently successful in these roles are probably already good at such tasks. Human analysts are important in the problem-solving process, and their input is likely to be even more important as the world drives toward big data and automated statistical learning.

End Notes

Introduction

1. Charlie Osborne, "Fortune 1000 to 'Urgently' Invest in Big Data, AI in 2019 in Fear of Digital Rivals," ZDNet, January 3, 2019, https://www.zdnet.com/article/fortune-1000-to-urgently-invest-in-big-data-ai-in-2019-in-fear-of-digital-rivals/.

Chapter 1

2. IBM. "Big Data Analytics," accessed May 9, 2021, https://www.ibm.com/analytics/hadoop/big-data-analytics.

3. S. Ransbotham, D. Kiron, and P.K. Prentice, "Beyond the Hype: The Hard Work Behind Analytics Success," MIT *Sloan Management Review*, March 2016.

4. Pranav Dar, "25 Open Datasets for Deep Learning Every Data Scientist Must Work With," *Analytics Vidhya*, March 29, 2018, https://www.analyticsvidhya.com/blog/2018/03/comprehensive-collection-deep-learning-datasets/.

5. Priya Pedamkar, "Big Data vs Data Science," *Educba*, accessed April 21, 2021, https://www.educba.com/big-data-vs-data-science/.

6. "Deep Learning: What It Is and Why It Matters," SAS, accessed April 21, 2021, https://www.sas.com/en_us/insights/analytics/deep-learning.html.

7. "Deep Learning," Nvidia.com, accessed June 2, 2021, https://developer.nvidia.com/deep-learning.

8. "Quality 4.0." Adapted from "Let's Get Digital" (*Quality Progress*), "The Ascent of Quality 4.0" (*Quality Progress*), and "Ahead of the Curve" (*Quality Progress*). Quality 4.0 study by Boston Consulting Group (BCG), American Society for Quality (ASQ), and Deutsche Gesellschaft für Qualität (DGQ), accessed April 21, 2021, https://asq.org/quality-resources/quality-4-0.

9. Quora, "What are the Risks and Benefits of Artificial Intelligence?" *Forbes.com*, August 2, 2019, https://www.forbes.com/sites/quora/2019/08/02/what-are-the-risks-and-benefits-of-artificial-intelligence/#489332ce34d8.

10. Gareth James, Daniella Witten, Trevor Hastie, and Robert Tibshirani, *An Introduction to Statistical Learning: With Applications in R* (Springer, 2013).

11. Kelly Terez and Brad Mielke, "Google Maps shortcut in Colorado turns into 'muddy mess' with 'a hundred cars,'" ABC News, June 26, 2019, https://abcnews.go.com/US/google-maps-shortcut-colorado-turns-muddy-mess-hundred/story?id=63946068.

12. Lauren Hansen, "8 drivers who blindly followed their GPS into disaster," The Week, May 7, 2013, https://theweek.com/articles/464674/8-drivers-who-blindly-followed-gps-into-disaster.

Chapter 2

13. John Koon, "Smart Sensor Applications in Manufacturing," Enterprise IoT Insights, August 27, 2018, https://enterpriseiotinsights.com/20180827/channels/fundamentals/iotsensors-smart-sensor-applications-manufacturing.

14. Cathy O'Neil, Weapons of Math Destruction: How Big Data Increases Inequality and Threatens Democracy (Crown, 2016).

Chapter 3

15. Yiran Dong and Chao-Ying Joanne Peng, "Principled Missing Data Methods for Researchers," PMC, 2013, accessed April 3, 2021, https://www.ncbi.nlm.nih.gov/pmc/articles/PMC3701793/.

16. Mark Allen Durivage, Practical Design of Experiments: A Guide for Optimizing Designs and Processes (Quality Press, 2016).

17. Dr. Saul McLeod, "Introduction to the Normal Distribution (Bell Curve)," Simply Psychology, 2019, accessed June 19, 2021, https://www.simplypsychology.org/normal-distribution.html.

Chapter 4

18. UCLA: Statistical Consulting Group, "Multiple Imputation in SAS Part 1," accessed May 11, 2021, https://stats.idre.ucla.edu/sas/seminars/multiple-imputation-in-sas/mi_new_1/.

19. Donald B. Rubin, "Inference and Missing Data," Biometrika, Volume 63, Issue 3, December 1976, Pages 581–592, accessed May 8, 2021, https://doi.org/10.1093/biomet/63.3.581.

20. Ibid.

21. "Statsmodels.imputation.mice.MICE," accessed June 2, 2021, https://www.statsmodels.org/stable/generated/statsmodels.imputation.mice.MICE.html.

Chapter 5

22. Jonathan Taylor, "Statistics 202: Data Mining," 2012, accessed May 2, 2021, http://statweb.stanford.edu/~jtaylo/courses/stats202/restricted/notes/trees.pdf.

23. SAS *Institute*, "Testing for Autocorrelation," 1999, accessed May 11, 2021, https://v8doc.sas.com/sashtml/ets/chap8/sect5.htm.

Chapter 6

24. Jason Brownlee, "A Gentle Introduction to Statistical Sampling and Resampling," Machine Learning Mastery, last updated August 8, 2019, https://machinelearningmastery.com/statistical-sampling-and-resampling/.

25. Isabelle Albert, Sophie Donnet, Chantal Guihenneuc-Jouyaux, Samantha Lowchoy, Kerrie Mengersen, and Judith Rousseau, "Combining Expert Opinions in Prior Elicitation," *Bayesian Analysis*, 7. 10.1214/12-BA717, https://www.researchgate.net/publication/254212803_Combining_Expert_Opinions_in_Prior_Elicitation.

26. "Three Conjugate Families," *An Introduction to Bayesian Thinking*: A *Companion to the Statistics with R Course*. https://statswithr.github.io/book/bayesian-inference.html#three-conjugate-families.

27. Judea Pearl, Madelyn Glymour, and Nicholas P. Jewell, *Causal Inference in Statistics: A Primer* (Wiley, 2009).

Chapter 7

28. William Q. Meeker, "Reliability: The Other Dimension of Quality," ASQ *Statistics Division Newsletter*, Vol. 21, No. 2, accessed May 11, 2021, http://asq.org/statistics/continuous-improvement/reliability-the-other-dimension-of-quality.pdf.

Chapter 8

29. Jason Brownlee, "How to Remove Outliers for Machine Learning," *Machine Learning Mastery*, last updated August 18, 2020, https://machinelearningmastery.com/how-to-use-statistics-to-identify-outliers-in-data/.

30. Information Technology Laboratory, NIST, accessed May 11, 2021, https://www.itl.nist.gov/div898/handbook/eda/section3/eda35h.html.

31. "Multiple Comparions," San Francisco State University, accessed June 2, 2021, http://online.sfsu.edu/efc/classes/biol458/multcomp/multcomp.htm.

Glossary

Acceptance sampling: Inspection of a sample from a lot to decide whether to accept that lot. There are two types: attributes sampling and variables sampling. In attributes sampling, the presence or absence of a characteristic is noted in each of the units inspected. In variables sampling, the numerical magnitude of a characteristic is measured and recorded for each inspected unit; this involves reference to a continuous scale of some kind.

American Society for Quality (ASQ): A professional, not-for-profit association that develops, promotes and applies quality-related information and technology for the private sector, government and academia. ASQ serves individual and organizational members in more than 140 countries.

Analytics: Data-intensive methods for business.

Average chart: A control chart in which the subgroup average, X-bar, is used to evaluate the stability of the process level.

Average sample number (ASN): The average number of sample units inspected per lot when reaching decisions to accept or reject.

Baseline measurement: The beginning point, based on an evaluation of output over a period of time, used to determine the process parameters prior to any improvement effort; the basis against which change is measured.

Bayes' theorem: A formula to calculate conditional probabilities by relating the conditional and marginal probability distributions of random variables.

Bias: The difference between the observed large sample average and the population mean.

Big data: An approach utilizing very large and rich data repositories.

Binomial distribution: Probability distribution for two discrete outcomes with replacement.

Calibration: The comparison of a measurement instrument or system of unverified accuracy to a measurement instrument or system of known accuracy to detect any variation from the required performance specification.

Centerline: A line on a graph that represents the overall average (mean) operating level of the process.

Censoring: Hiding of information from a variable A due to observed values of a second variable B.

Chain sampling plan: In acceptance sampling, a plan in which the criteria for acceptance and rejection apply to the cumulative sampling results for the current lot and one or more immediately preceding lots.

Chart: A tool for organizing, summarizing, and depicting data in graphic form.

Combinatorics: Mathematics of counting for complex sets.

Continuous sampling plan: In acceptance sampling, a plan, intended for application to a continuous flow of individual units of product, that involves acceptance and rejection on a unit-by-unit basis and employs alternate periods of 100% inspection and sampling. The relative amount of 100% inspection depends on the quality of submitted product. Continuous sampling plans usually require that each t period of 100% inspection be continued until a specified number, i, of consecutively inspected units are found clear of defects. Note: For single-level continuous sampling plans, a single d sampling rate (for example, inspect one unit in five or one unit in 10) is used during sampling. For multilevel continuous sampling plans, two or more sampling rates can be used. The rate at any time depends on the quality of submitted product.

Control chart: A time-sequenced chart with upper and lower control limits on which values of some statistical measure for a series of samples or subgroups are plotted. The chart frequently shows a centerline to help detect a trend of plotted values toward either control limit.

Control limits: The natural boundaries of a process within specified confidence levels, expressed as the upper control limit (UCL) and the lower control limit (LCL).

Correlation (statistical): A measure of the relationship between two data sets of variables.

Count chart: A control chart for evaluating the stability of a process in terms of the count of events of a given classification occurring in a sample; known as a c chart.

Count per unit chart: A control chart for evaluating the stability of a process in terms of the average count of events of a given classification per unit occurring in a sample, known as a u chart.

Cp: The ratio of tolerance to 6 sigma, or the upper specification limit (USL) minus the lower specification limit (LSL) divided by 6 sigma. It is sometimes referred to as the engineering tolerance divided by the natural tolerance and is only a measure of dispersion.

Cumulative sum control chart (CUSUM): A control chart on which the plotted value is the cumulative sum of deviations of successive samples from a target value. The ordinate of each plotted point represents the algebraic sum of the previous ordinate and the most recent deviations from the target.

Data: A set of collected facts. There are two basic kinds of numerical data: measured or variable data, such as "16 ounces," "4 miles" and "0.75 inches"; and counted or attribute data, such as "162 defects."

Data collection and analysis: The process to determine what data are to be collected, how the data are collected, and how the data are to be analyzed.

Data collection and analysis tools: A set of tools that help with data collection and analysis. These tools include check sheets, spreadsheets, histograms, trend charts, and control charts.

Discrete uniform sampling: A sampling of discrete, or separate and distinct, outcomes with equal probabilities for all values.

Failure mode analysis (FMA): A procedure to determine which malfunction symptoms appear immediately before or after a failure of a critical parameter in a system or product. After all possible causes are listed for each symptom, the product is designed to eliminate the problems.

Failure mode effects analysis (FMEA): A systematized group of activities to recognize and evaluate the potential failure of a product or process and its effects, identify actions that could eliminate or reduce the occurrence of the potential failure and document the process.

Frequency distribution (statistical): A table that graphically presents a large volume of data so the central tendency (such as the average or mean) and distribution are clearly displayed.

Hazard analysis and critical control point (HACCP): A quality management system for effectively and efficiently ensuring farm-to-table food safety in the United States. HACCP regulations for various sectors are established by the Department of Agriculture and the Food and Drug Administration.

Hyper-geometric distribution: Probability distribution for sampling two discrete outcomes without replacement.

In-control process: A process in which the statistical measure being evaluated is in a state of statistical control; in other words, the variations among the observed sampling results can be attributed to a constant system of chance causes. Also see "out-of-control process."

In-line systems: Measurement systems that have components embedded in the production process.

Inspection: A verification activity. For example, measuring, examining, testing, and gauging one or more characteristics of a product or service and comparing the results with specified requirements to determine whether conformity is achieved for each characteristic.

Inspection lot: A collection of similar units or a specific quantity of similar material offered for inspection and acceptance at one time.

International Organization for Standardization (ISO): An independent, nongovernmental international organization with a membership of 161 national standards bodies that unites experts to share knowledge and develop voluntary, consensus-based, market-relevant international standards, guidelines, and other types of documents.

Lot size (also referred to as N): The number of units in a lot.

Lower control limit (LCL): Control limit for points below the centerline in a control chart.

Matrix: A document for displaying the relationships among various data sets.

Mean: A measure of central tendency; the arithmetic average of all measurements in a data set.

Median: The middle number or center value of a set of data in which all the data are arranged in sequence.

Metric: A standard for measurement.

Mode: The value occurring most frequently in a data set.

Multivariate control chart: A control chart for evaluating the stability of a process in terms of the levels of two or more variables or characteristics.

n: The number of units in a sample.

N: The number of units in a population.

Normal distribution (statistical): The charting of a data set in which most of the data points are concentrated around the average (mean), thus forming a bell-shaped curve.

Operating characteristic curve (OC curve): A graph to determine the probability of accepting lots as a function of the lots' or processes' quality level when using various sampling plans. There are three types: type A curves, which give the probability of acceptance for an individual lot coming from finite production (will not continue in the future); type B curves, which give the probability of acceptance for lots coming from a continuous process; and type C curves, which (for a continuous sampling plan) give the long-run percentage of product accepted during the sampling phase.

Out-of-control process: A process in which the statistical measure being evaluated is not in a state of statistical control. In other words, the variations among the observed sampling results cannot be attributed to a constant system of chance causes. Also see "in-control process."

Percent chart: A control chart for evaluating the stability of a process in terms of the percentage of the total number of units in a sample in which an event of a given classification occurs. Also referred to as a proportion chart.

Poisson distribution: A discrete probability distribution that expresses the probability of a number of events occurring in a fixed time period if these events occur with a known average rate, and are independent of the time since the last event.

Probability (statistical): The likelihood of occurrence of an event, action, or item.

Process capability: A statistical measure of the inherent process variability of a given characteristic.

Process capability index: The value of the tolerance specified for the characteristic divided by the process capability. The several types of process capability indexes include the widely used Cpk and Cp.

Proportion chart: See "percent chart."

Quality: A subjective term for which each person or sector has its own definition. In technical usage, quality can have two meanings: 1) the characteristics of a product or service that bear on its ability to satisfy stated or implied needs; 2) a product or service free of deficiencies.

Quality 4.0: Quality 4.0 brings together Industry 4.0's advanced digital technologies with quality excellence to drive substantial performance and effectiveness improvements.

Quality assurance/quality control (QA/QC): Two terms that have many interpretations because of the multiple definitions for the words "assurance" and "control." One definition of quality assurance is: all the planned and systematic activities implemented within the quality system that can be demonstrated to provide confidence that a product or service will fulfill requirements for quality. One definition for quality control is: the operational techniques and activities used to fulfill requirements for quality.

Quality tool: An instrument or technique to support and improve the activities of quality management and improvement.

Random cause: A cause of variation due to chance and not assignable to any factor.

Random sampling: A commonly used sampling technique in which sample units are selected so all combinations of n units under consideration have an equal chance of being selected as the sample.

Range (statistical): The measure of dispersion in a data set (the difference between the highest and lowest values).

Range chart (R chart): A control chart in which the subgroup range, R, evaluates the stability of the variability within a process.

Risk management: The identification, evaluation, and prioritization of risks to eliminate or mitigate their probability or severity or to leverage opportunities.

Root cause: A factor that caused a nonconformance and should be addressed with corrective action.

Root cause analysis: The method of identifying the cause of a problem, solving it, and preventing it from occurring again. Uncovering the correct and accurate reason(s) why something is happening or has already occurred.

Run chart: A chart showing a line connecting numerous data points collected from a process running over time.

Sample: In acceptance sampling, one or more units of product (or a quantity of material) drawn from a lot for purposes of inspection to reach a decision regarding acceptance of the lot.

Sample size [n]: The number of units in a sample.

Sample standard deviation chart (S chart): A control chart in which the subgroup standard deviation, s, is used to evaluate the stability of the variability within a process.

Sampling at random: As commonly used in acceptance sampling theory, the process of selecting sample units so all units under consideration have the same probability of being selected. Note: Equal probabilities are not necessary for random sampling; what is necessary is that the probability of selection be ascertainable. However, the stated properties of published sampling tables are based on the assumption of random sampling with equal probabilities. An acceptable method of random selection with equal probabilities is the use of a table of random numbers in a standard manner.

Sampling, double: Sampling inspection in which the inspection of the first sample leads to a decision to accept a lot, reject it, or take a second sample; the inspection of a second sample, when required, then leads to a decision to accept or reject the lot.

Sampling, multiple: Sampling inspection in which, after each sample is inspected, the decision is made to accept a lot, reject it, or take another sample. But there is a prescribed maximum number of samples, after which a decision to accept or reject the lot must be reached.

Sampling, single: Sampling inspection in which the decision to accept or reject a lot is based on the inspection of one sample.

Sampling, unit: Sequential sampling inspection in which, after each unit is inspected, the decision is made to accept a lot, reject it, or inspect another unit.

Scale parameter: A generic distribution parameter associated with the width of a distribution.

Scatter diagram: A graphical technique to analyze the relationship between two variables. Two sets of data are plotted on a graph, with the y-axis being used for the variable to be predicted and the x-axis being used for the variable to make the prediction.

Screening experiment: A recipe that can be used to specify combinations of conditions that enable the experimenter to use a single study to gain a valuable characterization of the relationship of process outputs to the studied factors.

Standard: The metric, specification, gauge, statement, category, segment, grouping, behavior, event, or physical product sample against which the outputs of a process are compared and declared acceptable or unacceptable. Also, documents that provide requirements, specifications, guidelines, or characteristics that can be used to ensure that materials, products, processes, and services are fit for their purpose.

Standard deviation (statistical): A computed measure of variability indicating the spread of the data set around the mean.

Standardization: When policies and common procedures are used to manage processes throughout the system.

Statistical process control (SPC): The application of statistical techniques to control a process; often used interchangeably with the term "statistical quality control" (see listing).

Statistical quality control (SQC): The application of statistical techniques to control quality. Often used interchangeably with the term "statistical process control" (see listing), although statistical quality control includes acceptance sampling, which statistical process control does not.

Statistics: A field that involves tabulating, depicting, and describing data sets; a formalized body of techniques characteristically involving attempts to infer the properties of a large collection of data from inspection of a sample of the collection.

Tampering: Action taken to compensate for variation within the control limits of a stable system; tampering increases rather than decreases variation, as evidenced in the funnel experiment.

Total quality control (TQC): A system that integrates quality development, maintenance, and improvement of the parts of an organization. It helps an organization economically manufacture its product and deliver its services.

Total quality management (TQM): A term first used to describe a management approach to quality improvement.. Simply put, it is a management approach to long-term success through customer satisfaction. TQM is based on all members of an organization participating in improving processes, products, services, and the culture in which they work.

Trend control chart: A control chart in which the deviation of the subgroup average, X-bar, from an expected trend in the process level is used to evaluate the stability of a process.

T-test: A method to assess whether the means of two groups are statistically different from each other.

Type I error: An incorrect decision to reject something (such as a statistical hypothesis or a lot of products) when it is acceptable.

Type II error: An incorrect decision to accept something when it is unacceptable.

U chart: Count-per-unit chart.

Unit: An object for which a measurement or observation can be made; commonly used in the sense of a "unit of product," the entity of product inspected to determine whether it is defective or nondefective.

Upper control limit (UCL): Control limit for points above the centerline in a control chart.

Validation: The act of confirming a product or service meets the requirements for which it was intended.

Validity: The ability of a feedback instrument to measure what it was intended to measure; also, the degree to which inferences derived from measurements are meaningful.

Variable data: Measurement information. Control charts based on variable data include average (X-bar) chart, range (R) chart, and sample standard deviation (s) chart (see individual listings).

Variation: A change in data, characteristic, or function caused by one of four factors: special causes, common causes, tampering, or structural variation (see individual entries).

Weibull: Widely used probability distribution for failure times or life spans.

X-bar chart: Average chart.

Zero defects: A performance standard and method Philip B. Crosby developed; states that if people commit themselves to watching details and avoiding errors, they can move closer to the goal of zero defects.

Index

Note: Page numbers in *italics* indicate figures and tables.

About the Author

Dr. William Mawby has a B.S. in natural systems from the Defiance College and a Ph.D. in biomathematics from North Carolina State University. He has completed research internships at Argonne National Laboratory and Roswell Park Memorial Hospital. Dr. Mawby retired in July 2016 from Michelin Americas Research and Development Corporation after 31 years of service as head of statistical services for North America. He has completed extensive consulting, teaching, and project experience for manufacturing, R&D, and commercial divisions and has taught more than 200 courses on many subjects in statistics and mathematics.

In addition to more than 30 patents (granted or in application), Dr. Mawby has written four technical books published by Quality Press. He is currently writing, teaching courses on climate change and big data, and volunteering at the American Association for the Advancement of Science and the Union of Concerned Scientists.

WHY ASQ?

ASQ is a global community of people passionate about quality, who use the tools, their ideas and expertise to make our world work better. ASQ: The Global Voice of Quality.

FOR INDIVIDUALS

Advance your career to the next level of excellence.

ASQ offers you access to the tools, techniques and insights that can help distinguish an ordinary career from an extraordinary one.

FOR ORGANIZATIONS

Your culture of quality begins here.

ASQ organizational membership provides the invaluable resources you need o concentrate on product, service and experiential quality and continuous mprovement for powerful top-line and bottom-line results.

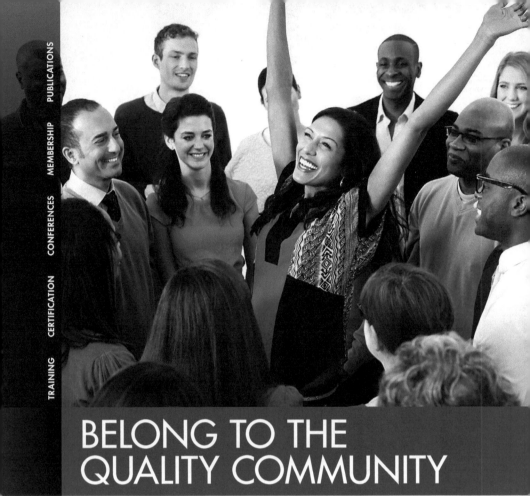